SHIPS IN FOCUS
Burns and Laird
Colin Campbell and Roy Fenton

Ships in Focus Publications

Published in the UK in 1999 by Ships in Focus Publications,
18 Franklands, Longton
Preston PR4 5PD

Printed by Amadeus Press Ltd., Huddersfield.
ISBN 1 901703 07 X

Front cover:	LAIRDS LOCH (see page 74) *[Malcolm Donelly]*
Title page:	ROYAL ULSTERMAN on trials 12th June 1936 (see page 65) *[Ulster Folk and Transport Museum 8003]*
Front end papers:	AZALEA of 1878 (see page 11) *[Glasgow University Archives]*
Rear end papers left:	the cargo and livestock motorships LAIRDSCREST, LAIRDSWOOD, and LAIRDSBANK, at Harland and Wolff's Queen's Island yard on 26th June 1936 (see pages 68-69). The other vessel, right front, is Bank Line's ERNEBANK (5,388/1937). *[Ulster Folk and Transport Museum 8012]*
Rear end papers right:	the impressive funnels of LAIRDS ISLE (see pages 60-61) *[Glasgow Transport Museum]*

FOREWORD

This book originated when Colin Campbell sent the publishers some photographs of Burns and Laird ships between the wars, asking whether they would make an article for *Ships in Focus Record*. It soon became clear that his collection, with additions from other sources, would make not just an article but a whole book on Burns and Laird. Colin then searched out other photographs from archives and collections on the west coast of Scotland so successfully that it seemed a shame to limit the book to the ships owned since the joint company was formed in 1922. We therefore decided to include photographs of any ships we could find belonging to the constituents. With companies who claimed origins at least a century before the amalgamation, it was never going to be possible to illustrate all their ships. This book is therefore best considered as a largely-complete photographic record of the ships of Burns and Laird Lines Ltd., which includes many ships from its constituents which did not survive until the amalgamation. We have also shown a selection of Burns and Laird ships in other owner's colours.

To new readers of our books, we should point out that our primary intention is to show photographically how the ships of a company developed. The captions give details of builders, engines and basic dimensions, and then describe the ship's career, discussing its place in history and pointing out any major excitements. To avoid the captions becoming too detailed, they do not include every change of owner but do note all subsequent or previous names, together with details of fates and other noteworthy events. The brief history of Burns and Laird and its constituents which follows this introduction is intended to place the companies in their historical context.

Reading various accounts of the histories of the companies which came together to make Burns and Laird suggests that the last word has certainly not been written on these owners and their pioneering role in developing British coastal and short sea steamship services. A modern shipping historian would have a rare old time investigating sources now available, sorting out the conflicting claims of earlier writers, and deciding the precise relationships of agents who advertised services and the individuals who owned the steamers. As compiling this book has convinced the authors, pioneers such as George Burns and Alexander Laird were often characters whose personalities remain vivid today, almost two centuries since they set up in business.

John Clarkson   Roy Fenton
Series editors, September 1999

A view from the entrance to Kingston Dock shows two Clyde Navigation Trust ferries together with Coast Lines' IRISH COAST and her sister SCOTTISH COAST on the Dublin berths at Anderston Quay and ROYAL SCOTSMAN on the Belfast berth at Lancefield Quay. IRISH COAST was never in Burns and Laird's ownership, but sailed frequently on their Glasgow-Dublin service.

BURNS AND LAIRD

During the 1950s a Sunday afternoon stroll along Glasgow's Broomielaw would take you past a large proportion of the fleet of Burns and Laird Lines. Starting at Berth 16 there would usually be the LAIRDSFERN, followed by the LAIRDS BEN and the LAIRDS MOOR being cleaned after discharging their loads of cattle from Londonderry and Dublin at Merklands Lairage. Then you could expect to see two Londonderry regulars: the cargo ship LAIRDSCREST and the passenger ship LAIRDS LOCH and, before crossing the arched walkway over the Clyde Street ferry, the LAIRDSGLEN at her Anderston Quay berth. Next would come the LAIRDSHILL at the Dublin berth, and finally the ROYAL SCOTSMAN at Lancefield Quay on her only day off. Today this whole area has been landscaped. The sheds have long gone, the walkway is seldom used, and the central area is dominated by the high level Kingston Bridge.

As the name infers, Burns and Laird Lines Ltd. was an amalgamation of two old-established Glasgow shipping companies. When the two companies came together in 1922 both had been in existence for over a century, and both had pioneered the Scotland to Ireland cross-channel trades. Laird Line came under the Coast Lines umbrella in October 1919, followed by G. and J. Burns Ltd. shortly afterwards. Burns and Laird Lines Ltd. was the logical outcome, a title formally adopted on 25th July 1922.

G. and J. Burns

Both constituent companies were amongst the world's oldest operators of steamships, and there is a suggestion that George Burns actually witnessed one of the first commercial sailings by a steamship, the departure of Henry Bell's COMET from Glasgow in 1812. Burns was one of the great pioneering figures of steam shipping, his influence going well beyond the cross-channel and coasting services which carried his name.

George and his elder brother James were produce merchants in Glasgow, and became interested in shipping around 1824. Sources differ on the exact order of events, but James and George Burns involved themselves in running the steamer AYR (75/1821) between Glasgow and Ayr; became agents for interests in Belfast which in 1825 planned a steamer service to the Clyde; and became Glasgow agents for a line of sailing smacks running to Liverpool, quickly becoming part owners of six of the smacks. Within a few months, Burns had thus laid the foundations of the three services which were to be the basis of the company's long-term success.

In March 1829 George Burns and his partner Mathie successfully introduced steam to the Liverpool service with the GLASGOW (280/1828). Much has been made of the story that George Burns wished his steamer to sail on Saturdays, which meant the GLASGOW would be at sea on the sabbath. Burns therefore provided a chaplain, and some wit on the Broomielaw taunted her master about 'sailing in a steam chapel'. Through his involvement in the Liverpool trade, George Burns began a relationship with David MacIver of Liverpool and, although this does not seem to have always been a cordial one, it did lead to the foundation of one of the world's most famous shipping lines. In 1839, George Burns, David MacIver and Samuel Cunard signed an understanding with the British Government to carry mails fortnightly between Liverpool, Halifax and Boston; an agreement that led to the formation of the Cunard Line. Burns' steamer UNICORN (649/1836), built for the Liverpool and Glasgow service, is sometimes claimed to have pioneered Cunard sailings, leaving Liverpool on 16th May 1840, but although she took passengers and cargo across the Atlantic she was intended to be used locally from Halifax in conjunction with the sailings of large steamers. Evidence of the close connection between Burns and Cunard is the similarity of their houseflags: Burns having a rampant golden lion holding a globe on a blue ground (see back cover), Cunard using a similar lion on red.

With an extensive network of steam services on the west of Scotland, Burns and his then partner Martin looked east in 1832 and announced their intention of moving some of their steamers into the Dundee-London trade. This panicked the directors of the Dundee, Perth and London Shipping Company to hurriedly order its own steamers for this route, and Martin and Burns then withdrew, seemingly not to venture onto east coast routes again.

George Burns embraced steam shipping enthusiastically, but his brother James was content to remain a produce merchant, and in recognition of George's primacy the title G. and J. Burns was adopted in 1842. Burns' involvement with the Glasgow and Belfast service was initially as agents, but they became identified as owners of the steamers as the service grew in frequency from its initial twice-weekly sailings to three per week in 1828, four in 1844, and daily (except Sundays) from 1849. The inauguration of the almost daily service resulted from Burns' offer to carry the Royal Mail free of charge between Belfast and Greenock (they were carried by train between there and Glasgow), so bringing to an end the Admiralty Mail Packet service between Donaghadee and Portpatrick.

Since the AYR operated on the Clyde during the 1820s, Burns had also built up a substantial interest in local services around the west of Scotland, acquiring a number of other companies of which the most substantial was the Glasgow Castles Steam Packet Company. However, in 1851 these ships and services were sold, presumably to allow financial and management resources to be concentrated on the services to Belfast and Liverpool. The West Highland services passed to David Hutcheson and Co., a predecessor of David MacBrayne, so that Burns could also claim credit for helping in the formation of another well-known fleet.

For the latter part of the nineteenth century, G. and J. Burns concentrated on developing their services between Scotland and Ireland. The Belfast mail steamers, in particular, tended to be handsome, fast paddlers. Several, including the STAG (499/1853), GIRAFFE (677/1860) and the brand new FOX (540/1863), were sold for use as blockade runners in the American Civil War. The GIRAFFE had a designed speed of 20 knots, and was intended to make daily return trips across the Irish Sea. But this service never came up to expectations, the GIRAFFE proving incapable of maintaining such a speed in everyday service, and passengers showed little interest in daily return trips with limited time in Belfast. The offer by a Confederate agent to buy the ship was undoubtedly well received. A more lasting expansion was a service to Londonderry opened in March 1866. However, a service to Larne begun in 1878 to compete with local traders who built their own steamer was less successful, and Larne was eventually served by twice-weekly calls by vessels sailing between Greenock and Belfast. Another new route came through an acquisition: in 1882 G. and J. Burns bought the Ardrossan Shipping Company, operated by Robert Henderson and Son, and with it a daily Ardrossan to Belfast service. Taking the story forward a few years, the company completed its network of Irish services with the 1908 take-over of the Dublin and Glasgow Sailing and Steam Packet Company and their four ships. The title of the Dublin company was changed to the Burns Steamship Co. Ltd. The parent company had adopted limited liability status in 1904, becoming G. and J. Burns Ltd.

Although the more glamorous vessels were built for the passenger and mail service to Belfast (slower, cargo-only vessels being built to run alongside them), the Liverpool service remained important. Until 1895 it was operated in conjunction with MacIvers, who were Liverpool agents, but following a disagreement which may have been precipitated by the opening of the Manchester Ship Canal, the companies ran in opposition, MacIvers buying two of Burns' older steamers for their service. Burns did grasp the opportunity presented by the Canal, and added ships for a Glasgow to Manchester service which carried cargo and steerage passengers, as well as building passenger-cargo ships for the Liverpool route.

Sir George Burns, founder of the company, died in 1890, and was succeeded as chairman of the company by his son John, who was to become Lord Inverclyde. He died in 1919, and on his death a company which had been highly acquisitive during its 95-year existence was itself acquired by Coast Lines Ltd.

Laird Line

Although given an inferior position in the title of the joint company, the Laird Line could claim seniority over G. and J. Burns in its longevity. This was based on the formation in 1814 of a company to provide steamer services connecting ports on the Clyde between Greenock and Inverary. The moving spirit in this company is generally agreed to be a Lewis MacLellan, who had been associated with Henry Bell and his steamer COMET. The earliest steamers operated by MacLellan's company were the BRITANNIA (73/1815) and WATERLOO (90/1816). The Clyde services were gradually extended, and in 1820 BRITANNIA sailed from the Clyde to the Giant's Causeway. Although the logical outcome of this excursion, a regular Clyde-Belfast service, was tried in 1821 and failed, sailings to Londonderry eventually became permanent, under the title Glasgow and Londonderry Steam Packet Company.

Although some writers involve Alexander Laird in these ventures from the outset, the more cautious merely state that he was a shipbroker who in 1822 became the Greenock agent for the St. George Steam Packet Company. The significance of Greenock was that, before the Upper Clyde was dredged, it was the nearest to Glasgow that seagoing vessels could berth at most states of the tide. Laird added an agency for the Mersey and Clyde Steam Navigation Company in 1823, and in 1825 began a service between Glasgow and Inverness. He was also associated with services from Greenock to Dublin, begun in 1826, to Newry in 1834, and to Dundalk in 1844.

Laird's dynamism and willingness to become involved with the growing network of steamer services makes it likely that he was already involved with the Glasgow and Londonderry Steam Packet Company, but it was to be many years before his company's name was formally linked with it. Meanwhile services were now extended to other ports in the north and west of Ireland, including Coleraine, Portrush, Sligo, Westport and Ballina, and to Glasgow itself. In 1843 a service was added from Liverpool to Sligo, and although this was given up in 1867 when the competing Sligo Steam Navigation Company agreed to cease its Glasgow to Sligo service, it returned to Laird's successor in the 1930s. A lasting institution was the use of plant names begun by the first SHAMROCK (636/1847).

In 1868 Alexander A. Laird and Co. became the sole Glasgow agents for the Glasgow and Londonderry company, this Laird being the son of the founder and who had joined the company in 1824. From this time on Lairds are increasingly referred to as owners of the steamers rather than as agents, and the title Laird Line was gradually adopted for the service.

A significant further absorption by Alexander A. Laird and Co. was the partnership of McConnell and Laird in 1873. This Laird seems to have been a brother of Alexander A. Laird. From 1853 his partnership ran a service between Glasgow and Londonderry which competed with the Glasgow and Londonderry Steam Packet Company, and later added services to Dublin and Portrush. Duckworth and Langmuir state that the Laird Line funnel - divided equally red, white and black - derived from a combination of the red funnel with black top inherited from a previous agent for the Glasgow and Londonderry company and McConnell and Laird's white funnel with black top. The latter funnel was a relic of the St. George Steam Packet Company.

The heady pioneering days of steam navigation on coastal and cross channel routes were over by 1867, and Lairds' course was now one of consolidation, with the building of progressively larger ships and the take-over of just one other company. In 1885 the concern which owned many of the steamers was incorporated as a limited company, becoming the Glasgow, Dublin and Londonderry Steam Packet Co. Ltd. Not all the ships were registered under this title, however, and the owners of some of the vessels operating Laird services between England and Ireland remained Alexander Laird and Co. and the children of MacLellan, whose family were also shareholders in the 1885 company. The England to Ireland services included Morecambe and Dublin and Morecambe and Londonderry operated in conjunction with the Midland Railway, and which moved to Heysham in 1904. A service between Fleetwood and Londonderry was run in conjunction with the Lancashire and Yorkshire Railway until 1903, and a weekly service from Liverpool to Larne, Coleraine and Westport. The unwieldiness of the Glasgow, Dublin and Londonderry name led to the adoption of Laird Line Ltd. in 1906, reflecting the title popularly used for many years.

Laird's last acquisition was the Ayr Steam Shipping Co. Ltd. in May 1908. Apart from adoption of Laird funnel colours, its ships retained their names and ownership by the Ayr company until absorption into Laird Line Ltd. in 1921. This was a tidying-up operation by the new owners, Laird Line Ltd. and Ayr Steam Shipping Co. Ltd. having become part of the Coast Lines group when an offer of £933,080 had been accepted in 1919.

Amalgamation

Initially, the Burns and Laird companies co-existed under Coast Lines ownership, but in 1922 the logical merger occurred, and Burns and Laird Lines Ltd. came into being on 25th July 1922. G. and J. Burns Ltd. contributed 15 ships to the new company: CONEY, GORILLA, GROUSE, HOUND, LURCHER, MAGPIE, MOORFOWL, PARTRIDGE, POINTER, PUMA, REDBREAST, SABLE, TIGER, VULTURE and WOODCOCK. Ten vessels were taken over from Laird Line Ltd.: BRIER, CAIRNSMORE, CULZEAN, DUNURE, LILY, MAPLE, OLIVE, ROSE, THISTLE and TURNBERRY. In a spirit of rationalisation, Coast Lines Ltd. transferred its Mersey to Glasgow trade to the new company, a service which was initially operated under the Burns-Langlands title.

After the amalgamation all the ships of the new company adopted the Laird Line funnel of equal parts of white and red with a black top, and the Burns houseflag of a golden lion on a blue ground.

The 1920s was not an auspicious decade for Burns and Laird, as the Burns constituent had lost some of its best ships in the First World War, whilst Laird, although coming off lighter, had seen its biggest steamer ROWAN sunk in collision during

A classic scene from the summers of the thirties, when the decks of departing Burns and Laird vessels were often packed with humanity. LAIRDSGLEN of 1914, ex MAPLE, leaves Glasgow for Londonderry in a rain shower on 17th July 1931. See page 41.

1922 with considerable loss of life and with blame largely attached to her master, who had gone down with his ship. If this was not enough, trade with Ireland - especially tourist traffic - had been hit by the troubles surrounding partition and home rule, and the constituents' fastest steamers, HAZEL and VIPER, were sold as a result. The merging of the two companies helped by allowing a rationalisation of services and of the ships required to cover them, and released some of the older units for sale. Although cargo vessels were built for the Clyde-Mersey service (and even these were transferred to Coast Lines Ltd. in 1925), no new passenger vessels joined the fleet for the 17 years from 1919 to 1936. The company's major service, the nightly Glasgow-Belfast sailings, was maintained by the WOODCOCK and PARTRIDGE which, if not chronologically old, were certainly dated. The Glasgow-Londonderry service was mainly in the hands of the even older OLIVE of 1893 and ROSE of 1902, whilst Glasgow-Dublin was still worked by the TIGER, built in 1906 for Burns' predecessor on the route, the Dublin and Glasgow Sailing and Steam Packet Company.

In 1929 it was decided to rename all the remaining fleet of 16 ships with the prefix LAIRDS-. This suggests the dead hand of Sir Alfred Read, moving spirit behind the formation of Coast Lines, but whose soulless corporate naming schemes also afflicted not only Coast Lines Ltd. itself but later Belfast Steamship Co. Ltd. Purists condemned the passing of the older Burns and Laird names, but when referring to them the LAIRD prefix was invariably dropped. The renamings were as follows:

BRIER	LAIRDSOAK
CONEY	LAIRDSFERRY
LILY	LAIRDSPOOL
MAGPIE	LAIRDSGROVE
MAPLE	LAIRDSGLEN
MOORFOWL	LAIRDSMOOR
OLIVE	LAIRDSBANK
PARTRIDGE	LAIRDSLOCH
POINTER	LAIRDSVALE
PUMA	LAIRDSFORD
ROSE	LAIRDSROSE
SABLE	LAIRDSELM
TIGER	LAIRDSFOREST
TURNBERRY	LAIRDSHEATHER
VULTURE	LAIRDSROCK
WOODCOCK	LAIRDSWOOD

The year 1929 also saw the fleet adopt a red funnel with black top in replacement of the old Laird Line funnel. This was a reversion to the funnel used by the Glasgow and Londonderry Steam Packet Co. prior to the adoption of the Laird Line funnel in 1867, but was shortlived. In 1936 a narrow blue band was added to separate the red and black.

Only at the beginning of the 1930s did the company seem to regain its energy, first with the transfer of three relatively new British and Irish steamers for its principal Glasgow-Belfast sailings, allowing older ships to be cascaded to the Londonderry and Dublin routes, and some veterans to be sold or scrapped. Then came the secondhand but spectacularly fast RIVIERA to revive the ailing

Ardrossan-Belfast service. She was a snip at just £4,100, but needed much work doing.

With the arrival of the sister ships ROYAL ULSTERMAN and ROYAL SCOTSMAN from Harland and Wolff in 1936 a completely new era dawned for the Glasgow-Belfast service. Burns and Laird now had state-of-the-art motor ferries every bit as good as those elsewhere on the Irish Sea, and indeed probably the equal of any in the world. Their arrival allowed further cascading of ships to the Dublin and Londonderry services, and their speed and performance permitted the night-time Ardrossan-Belfast sailings to be abandoned with further savings. However, cargo on this route was important, and soon after the ROYALs were delivered Burns and Laird's first motor cargo vessels arrived to inaugurate an Ayr-Ardrossan-Belfast service. Part of the finance for these ships came from a bank loan guaranteed by the Ministry of Finance for Northern Ireland, who were anxious to obtain work for the Belfast shipyard.

The company's most serious accident since the ROWAN disaster was the sinking of the LAIRDSMOOR in collision with Shaw Savill's TARANAKI in dense fog in April 1937 with the loss of her master and one fireman.

During the Second World War many of the company's vessels were requisitioned under the Liner Requisition Scheme, although remaining largely on their existing routes. However, the ROYAL ULSTERMAN and ROYAL SCOTSMAN were taken far from home, and after considerable adaptation served gallantly at a number of Allied landings. Remarkably, the company sustained no losses as a result of hostile action during the war, but lost one vessel, and almost lost two others, as a result of collisions: LAIRDSGLEN was damaged in 1939, LAIRDSCASTLE sank in 1941 fortunately without casualties, and KERRY COAST was beached in 1944. The loss of the LAIRDSCASTLE was compensated for by the wartime completion of LAIRDS LOCH, although she was intended to replace LAIRDSROSE on the Londonderry sailings.

With a numerically strong fleet, Burns and Laird were in an enviable position to take advantage of the post-war boom in trade. Although never one to spend freely, its Coast Lines parent did provide for its cargo and cattle-handling requirements, transferring suitable motor coasters for the important steel services into Harland and Wolff's shipyard, and investing in three new and one old cattle carriers.

In 1951 Coast Lines built the IRISH COAST whose primary purpose was to relieve all the Group's passenger ships to allow them to go for overhaul during the winter months. In 1953 this ship took over Burns and Laird's Glasgow-Dublin service during the summer months, and from 1961 she took over the Ardrossan-Belfast service from LAIRDS ISLE. The SCOTTISH COAST, a virtual sister to the IRISH COAST, was launched at Belfast in 1956. In July 1957 the SCOTTISH COAST took up the Glasgow-Dublin service. But the IRISH and SCOTTISH COAST, along with the two ROYALs of which they were essentially developments, had poor vehicle capacity, and by the early 1960s it was apparent that roll-on, roll-off was the future for both freight and most passengers. Burns and Laird's answer was the LION of 1967 for the Ardrossan-Belfast service. A one-class ship, she was able to carry 1,200 passengers and 160 cars all year round, and having both bow and stern doors was drive through. LION also took night sailings to and from Larne, but rumours abounded that she could be better used elsewhere, and this happened in 1976 when she was transferred to the English Channel. The last vestige of the old company disappeared later that year when the motor coaster LAIRDSFOX was given a pale blue P&O funnel.

The Coast Lines Group, huge and apparently unassailable in the early 1950s, withered away over the next two decades as a result of road competition on its purely coastwise routes and its seeming inability to take the initiative on roll-on, roll-off cross-channel services, although it did better on unit load services. Its Burns and Laird subsidiary, which should have been in a strong position because of its predominantly cross-channel trade, was infected by the same malaise and died with its parent. P&O, which inherited Coast Lines' Irish Sea services, did retain an echo of G. and J. Burns in names such as BISON, BUFFALO and POINTER given to its ships, but sadly these have now succumbed to an enthusiasm for EUROPEAN names.

This book is dedicated to preserving the memory of a famous company whose constituents were involved in the earliest days of steam navigation. Its forerunners supplied ministers on ships that sailed on Sundays, carried the mail free for more than 30 years, sold ships to the Confederate States and invested the moneys in bigger and faster ships, and built six-foot containers before the revolution.

The last Burns and Laird passenger vessel, LION noses her way into Ardrossan harbour during her trials: she is flying Cammell Laird's houseflag. See pages 90-91.

Sources and acknowledgements

A number of published and unpublished accounts of the early histories of G. and J. Burns and Alexander A. Laird and Co. have survived, mostly dated between about 1900 and the amalgamation in 1922. These have probably been compiled by successive managers or directors of the companies, and conflict in some details, although in others they agree word for word. Standing head and shoulders above these is the work of Duckworth and Langmuir, whose *Clyde and other Coastal Steamers* (Brown, Son and Ferguson, Glasgow 1939) is indeed a classic of shipping history, being cautious about reporting received wisdom, and clearly involving an enormous amount of work in researching individual ships and their careers.

Malcolm MacRonald most generously provided a fleet list of Burns and Laird Lines Ltd., which was much superior to those we were working from, and allowed our captions to be checked for accuracy. Other work on the ships' histories was carried out using the resources of the World Ship Society's Central Record and of Lloyd's Register of Shipping, and the *Registers* of Tony Starke and William Schell, the latter also kindly helping with some difficult fates.

Articles by Peter Myers and Malcolm MacRonald in *Marine News* for March and June 1997 gave full details of SCOTTISH COAST's career. Articles by Paul Clegg and others in *Sea Breezes* and *Ships Monthly* in the late 1960s did an excellent job of documenting the final, sad years of many Coast Lines services. *P&O: A Fleet History* by Stephen Rabson and Kevin O'Donoghue (World Ship Society, Kendal, 1988) gives histories of some of Burns and Laird's last vessels. Laurence Liddle, whilst inclined to lapse into anecdote and not check his facts, gives a useful route-by route account of passenger services in *Passenger Ships of the Irish Sea 1919-1969* (Colourpoint, Newtownards, 1998). Arnold Hague's *Convoy Rescue Ships* (World Ship Society, Gravesend, 1998) gave details of RATHLIN's wartime career. Minutes of Burns and Laird Ltd. were examined in Strathclyde Regional Archives.

Photographs not otherwise acknowledged are from the collections of the authors or John Clarkson. For help with obtaining photographs the publishers had the wholehearted support of many photographers, private collectors and administrators of large collections. We thank the Mitchell Library; Glasgow University Business Archives especially George Gardner; Tony Smith and David Whiteside of the World Ship Photo Library; David Hodge and colleagues at the National Maritime Museum; Bill Lind of the Ballast Trust; librarians and curators from most major libraries and museums in the West of Scotland; the Imperial War Museum; Paul Boot; Ambrose Greenway; Donald McColl; Peter Newall; William Schell; and George Scott. Last but not least we are most grateful to Louis Loughran who researched and drew the flags and funnels on the back cover, and to Charles Waine.

BURNS STEAMERS OF THE 1860s AND 1870s

PENGUIN (top)

Tod and McGregor, Meadowside; 1864, 749gt, 221 feet

2-cyl. by Tod and McGregor, Meadowside

During the 1860s, G. and J. Burns were ordering both screw and paddle steamers simultaneously. The paddlers were preferred for services where speed was important, particularly the Clyde-Belfast crossing, whilst screw steamers - with their better capacity - were used where there was more cargo than passengers. The screw steamer PENGUIN was built for the Clyde-Liverpool service but, because she had substantial passenger accommodation, was later moved to the Belfast service to supplement the paddlers.

In March 1878 PENGUIN was sold to the Union Steam Ship Co. Ltd. of New Zealand, for whom her name was particularly appropriate. She gave New Zealand 30 years' service, being wrecked off Cape Terawhiti on 12th February 1909 whilst on a voyage from Picton to Wellington. Her survival for so long in an area where ships were routinely photographed has enabled the inclusion of an excellent image of the oldest ship featured in this book. *[M.M. and S.W. Bond, courtesy Ballast Trust]*

BEAR (bottom)

J. and G. Thomson, Govan; 1870, 697gt, 221 feet

C. 2-cyl. by J. and G. Thomson, Govan

BEAR was notable as the first ship built for James Burns with a compound engine. Despite the pioneering nature of these engines, BEAR and other Burns' steamers of the 1870s were remarkably long-lived, reflecting not only their excellent

engineering, but also the lack of technological advances in coastal steamers over their half century of existence.

Although also used on Londonderry sailings, BEAR ran mainly in the company's Glasgow, Greenock and Liverpool services, which used the title Glasgow and Liverpool Steam Shipping Company, and for whom Liverpool agents were David MacIver and Co. In 1895, Burns relinquished this arrangement with the MacIvers, probably because it was felt that the opportunities offered by the opening of the Manchester Ship Canal merited a better service to the Mersey, and Burns reopened

an office in Liverpool. Somewhat surprisingly, the ageing BEAR, along with the OWL, was sold to a company managed by the MacIver family, the Liverpool and Clyde Steam Navigation Co. Ltd.

In 1903 BEAR was sold to Bell's Asia Minor Steamship Co. Ltd., and in 1909 became the CALYPSO of the Hellenic Steam Navigation Co. of Piraeus, managed by the English-sounding McDowall and Barbour. On 31st January 1914 CALYPSO was wrecked near the island of Paros while on a voyage from Piraeus to Santorin with general cargo. *[Glasgow University Archives, DC101/0059]*

FERRET (top)

J. and G. Thomson, Govan; 1871, 343gt, 171 feet
C. 2-cyl. by J. and G. Thomson, Govan

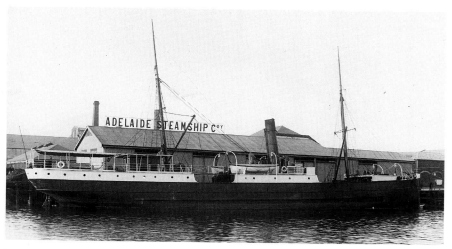

FERRET was the subject of one of the most daring and celebrated scams in shipping history. She was built for Burns' service between the Clyde and Belfast, making three sailings each week, but in 1873 was sold to the Dingwall and Skye Railway Company (later the Highland Railway Company) for a service between Strome Ferry and Portree.

In October 1880 an offer to charter FERRET was received from a Mr. Smith, who claimed to be related to W.H. Smith, the late First Lord of the Admiralty. He maintained that his wife had been ill and he wanted to take her on a six-month cruise in the Mediterranean. His references were checked and found satisfactory, and the first half-month's charter was paid in cash.

FERRET was currently at her builders for an overhaul, and runners were used to move her to Cardiff, where coaling was paid for with bills which later proved worthless. FERRET sailed on 25th October 1880, but needed to put in to Milford Haven because of bad weather, and left on 1st November for Marseilles. She never arrived. Passing through the Straits of Gibraltar on 11th November she made requests to be reported. Her white funnel was then repainted black, and all but two of her blue lifeboats were repainted white. Under cover of darkness she turned back through the Straits of Gibraltar, and the two blue lifeboats were thrown overboard. When she put in to St. Vincent in the Cape Verde Islands for water and stores her name had been changed to BENTON.

The ship arrived at Santos, Brazil on 20th December, declaring her voyage to be from Cape Town in ballast for England. She loaded a cargo of 3,992 bags of coffee for Marseilles and sailed on 11th January 1881, but arrived in Cape Town on 29th January where her cargo was sold for £11,000. After efforts were made to sell the ship, coal was loaded and she sailed on 14th February arriving at Mauritius on 1st March. After clearing for Guam, she then appeared in Port Albany in Western Australia, and then Melbourne. It was reported that her fires were always banked, ready to sail at a moment's notice, but she was seized by the Customs in Australia on 27th April 1881. 'Smith' and his wife, Captain Wright and Walker, the chief

steward, had all fled, but were subsequently arrested. Smith and Walker were given seven years penal servitude, and Wright three and a half years.

After these excitements, FERRET settled down to a more dignified career. She was purchased by the Adelaide Steam Ship Co. Ltd. and sailed on for almost 40 years, being wrecked near Cape Spencer on 11th November 1920 whilst carrying a general cargo from Port Adelaide to the Spencer Gulf ports. *[I.J. Farquhar collection]*

OWL (middle)

Tod and McGregor, Meadowside; 1873, 915gt, 230 feet
C. 2-cyl. by Tod and McGregor, Meadowside

The OWL was built for the Glasgow-Liverpool sailings and, like her running mate BEAR, was sold to the Liverpool and Clyde Steam Navigation Co. Ltd. in 1895. Both ships later went to Greek-based companies, OWL going to McDowall and Barbour in 1901 to become ANTIGONE. She later passed to the grandly-named Hellenic

Company of Maritime Enterprises. ANTIGONE leaves Lloyd's Register in 1928, probably being scrapped after over fifty years' service. *[Glasgow Museums]*

MASTIFF (bottom)

J. and G. Thomson, Clydebank; 1878, 871gt, 230 feet
C. 2-cyl. by J. and G. Thomson, Clydebank

MASTIFF and her sister WALRUS (not illustrated, 870/1878) were iron steamers with similar dimensions to OWL, but with shallower draft to allow passage of Belfast Lough at any state of the tide. MASTIFF stayed on the Glasgow-Belfast service until 1881, when she was transferred to the Londonderry route, also serving Liverpool and - after 1895 - Manchester.

MASTIFF was sold to M.H. Bland and Co. of Gibraltar in 1906 to become GIBEL DERSA. After a respectable second career with these owners, she left Gibraltar late in December 1923, arriving at Genoa to be broken up on 5th January 1924. *[Glasgow University Archives, DC101/0402]*

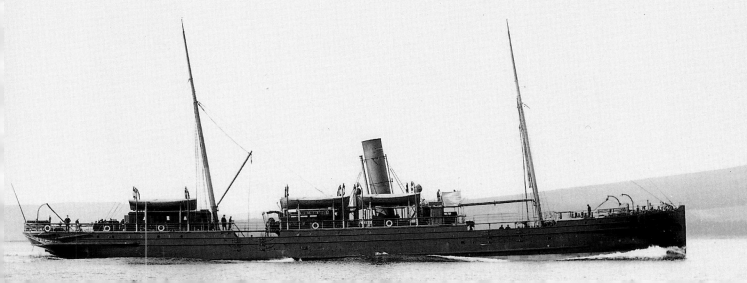

LAIRD STEAMERS OF THE 1860s AND 1870s

ROSE (2) (top)

Blackwood and Gordon, Port Glasgow; 1867, 409gt, 180 feet
C. 2-cyl. by Young and Co., Port Glasgow (new in 1872)

The oldest Laird vessel of which an acceptable photograph has been found is the screw steamer ROSE, posing off the Customs House, Dublin. Her minimalist superstructure - just an engine casing topped by an open bridge - her slim funnel, and the rakish angle of her masts date her to the early years of iron screw steamers. A plant name, which for many years distinguished all Alexander Laird's steamers, was an afterthought in her case, as she was launched as ERIN, and renamed ROSE to enter the Sligo service.

ROSE's early life was not trouble-free, as on 5th December 1869 she collided with the Anchor Line steamer CAMBRIA (2,141/1869) in the Firth of Clyde and had to be beached at Lamlash on Arran. ROSE was sold in 1883, but continued to run on the Irish Sea as AILSA, now owned by David Rowan the engine builder, and running for his Ayr Steam Shipping Co. Ltd. Many years later this company was bought and absorbed by Laird Line, but the end for AILSA came on 26th February 1892 when she was wrecked on Port Muck, Islandmagee whilst on a voyage from Ayr to Belfast with general cargo. *[Ambrose Greenway collection]*

HOLLY (bottom)

D. and W. Henderson and Co., Meadowside; 1875, 378gt, 170 feet
C. 2-cyl. by Thomas Wingate and Co.,

Whiteinch

Alexander Laird's early involvement with the St. George Steam Packet Company left a lasting legacy in the continued use of the latter company's funnel colours, white with black top, by certain ships trading between Glasgow and Dublin, as seen here on the HOLLY. McConnell and Laird had used this funnel until 1873, and it is said to have originated the white base used by Laird himself and by Burns and Laird until 1929.

Sold in 1893, HOLLY went to the eastern Mediterranean, where she was to be joined by many of her consorts. She first became PIRAEUS of La Navigation Héllénique, managed by A. Diakaki, subsequently becoming HALCYON and later SERIFOS for other Greek owners. She was broken up in 1935 after a remarkable 60 years'service: HOLLY was truly an evergreen. *[Glasgow University Archives, DC101/0291]*

AZALEA (top)

A. and J. Inglis, Pointhouse; 1878, 706gt, 218 feet

C. 2-cyl. by A. and J. Inglis, Pointhouse

The AZALEA was intended for Laird's Londonderry service, but ran to Dublin until the SHAMROCK was delivered in 1879. Along with her sister CEDAR (719/1878), AZALEA could carry 70 passengers.

After new, higher-pressure boilers were fitted in 1893, AZALEA's maximum speed was increased by half a knot, and she was transferred to the Gourock-Portrush daylight service, later opening the Ardrossan-Portrush daylight service with LILY. Her final service was on the Ayr-Belfast route, acquired with the Ayr Steam Shipping Co. Ltd. in 1908.

In 1914 AZALEA was sold to Navigation à Vapeur Ionienne (G. Yannoulatos Frères) and renamed first CHALKIS, and later NAFKRATOUSSA. In 1927 she moved to Coast Line Steamship Co. of Greece, and then in 1933 to Hellenic Coast Lines Ltd. who renamed her PSARA. She was sold for scrap in May 1939, after a monumental career. *[Clyde River Steamer Club 1125, courtesy D. McColl]*

SHAMROCK (2) (right)

A. and J. Inglis, Pointhouse; 1879, 832gt, 231 feet

C. 2-cyl. by A. and J. Inglis, Pointhouse

The SHAMROCK was built to carry 80 passengers on Laird's Glasgow-Dublin route, operating alongside the steamers of the Dublin and Glasgow Sailing and Steam Packet Company (see page 32). However, this photograph, taken at The Quays, Londonderry, establishes that she was not confined to this service.

After a long and relatively trouble-free career, during which she maintained the Glasgow-Dublin service during the First World War, she was wrecked in Freshwater Bay, Lambay Island, County Dublin on 5th May 1919 whilst on a voyage from Glasgow to Dublin with general cargo. *[National Library of Ireland]*

LAIRD STEAMERS OF THE 1880s

BRIER and **ENDA** (all on this page)
D. and W. Henderson and Co., Meadowside; 1882, 710gt, 210 feet
C. 2-cyl. by D. and W. Henderson and Co., Meadowside

With a summer capacity of 80 passengers, 285 cattle, and 8 horses, BRIER was employed first on the Glasgow-Londonderry service. But like other Laird vessels, she was cascaded onto other services during a career which spanned half a century. BRIER ran for a time to Portrush, then sailed from Ayr, and is known to have run between Morecambe (see below left) and Heysham and Londonderry.

When renamed along with the rest of the Burns and Laird fleet in 1929, the position of a porthole was such that her name appeared on one bow as LAIRD SOAK, and this was how she was subsequently known. In 1931 she was transferred to Michael Murphy Ltd. of Dublin for the paltry sum of £500 and renamed ENDA, but in 1933 was chartered back to Burns and Laird. This charter was shortlived as, on 27th February 1933 whilst on passage from Londonderry to Heysham, ENDA ran ashore at Clanyard Bay on the Mull of Galloway and became a total loss (bottom right). *[Top: Glasgow University Archives, DC101/0080; bottom left: Ambrose Greenway collection; bottom right: courtesy Peter Moir]*

DAPHNE (opposite page top)
Alexander Stephen and Sons, Linthouse; 1883, 449gt, 177 feet
C. 2-cyl. by Alexander Stephen and Sons, Linthouse

DAPHNE was one of those unfortunate ships whose name is associated with a major disaster. She was launched on 3rd July 1883 with her machinery on board, but with a large opening in her deck to enable her boilers to be installed. Once afloat, she listed and then turned over, with the loss of 124 lives. This huge number of men were on board because of the haste to complete her for service during the Glasgow Fair holiday in late July. With a disaster of such magnitude an enquiry was held, but this exonerated the builders from any blame for killing 124 of their employees on the grounds that stability calculations were not routinely made for new vessels.

The DAPHNE was raised but, because of the unfortunate association with her name, she became ROSE (3) when completed in September. But misfortune still dogged her: on 1st March 1884 ROSE ran ashore in fog at Farlane Point, Millport. After part of her cargo was discharged, she was refloated, but Lairds had clearly had enough of the vessel, and later that year she was sold to John Bell and Co. of Prestwick. As her new name IANTHE suggests, she was put into service in the eastern Mediterranean. In 1890 she was sold to Navigation Orientale and was renamed ELENI. She is believed to have been mined off Tenedos on 10th December 1918. *[D. McColl collection]*

ELM (middle)
A. and J. Inglis, Pointhouse; 1884, 489gt, 182 feet
C. 2-cyl. by A. and J. Inglis, Pointhouse
The ELM was the third steamer built for
Lairds in 1884, the other being the THISTLE
and the first DAISY (not illustrated, 216/1884),
which was sold after five years without,
apparently, any photographic record
surviving. Built of steel for the Gourock-
Portrush daylight service, ELM was also used
on services from Morecambe and later
Heysham to Londonderry or Dublin. For the
last of these services she was given a red
funnel with a black top, and this may explain
the non-standard colours in this photograph,
although the funnel could be a soot-stained,
uniform black.

In 1910 ELM was sold to Empreza de
Navigazion Bahiana, Bahia, Brazil and
renamed GAURARAPES. Her fate remains a
mystery: she drops out of *Lloyd's Register* in
1916 with no explanation, but does not figure
in the modest list of Brazilian losses during
the First World War. *[Glasgow Museums]*

THISTLE (5) (bottom)
D. and W. Henderson and Co., Meadowside;
1884, 803gt, 217 feet
C. 2-cyl. by D. and W. Henderson and Co.,
Meadowside
The first Laird Line ship constructed of steel,
THISTLE justified her owners' faith in the new
material and remained in service for 44 years,
sailing mainly between Londonderry and
Glasgow, Heysham or Fleetwood. Her
summer passenger certificate allowed for
564 passengers, but she appeared to have
only 43 sleeping berths. The all-important
walk on/walk off cattle and horses were
provided with 335 and 12 stalls, respectively.

The photograph shows THISTLE
after being lengthened to 231 feet in 1893.
She was never given a LAIRD- name, being
sold in December 1928 to be broken up by
Smith and Co. at Port Glasgow.

LAIRD STEAMERS OF THE 1880s (continued)

GARDENIA (top)
D. and W. Henderson and Co., Meadowside; 1885, 461gt, 172 feet
C. 2-cyl. by A. Stephen and Sons, Linthouse (built 1883)
With a strong family resemblance to the slightly larger ELM, GARDENIA was owned by Laird's somewhat ponderously-titled Glasgow, Dublin and Londonderry Steam Packet Co. Ltd. She served Londonderry, but perversely this photograph shows her in Coleraine in August 1898. Note the stern of the sailing ship to the right.

GARDENIA left the Laird fleet in 1904 when sold to an owner in Havre who did not rename her. She worked mainly in the Mediterranean, and was on a voyage from Marseilles to Nice when she foundered off Cannes on 8th November 1909. *[Peter Newall collection]*

IVY (bottom)
C.J. Bigger, Londonderry; 1888, 451gt, 190 feet
T. 3-cyl. by Lees, Anderson and Co., Glasgow
IVY was Laird's first ship with triple-expansion engines, built two years after Burns had adopted this type of machinery for HARE (see page 18). In 1890, IVY opened Laird's Greenock-Portrush daytime sailings, making two round trips each week, the return voyage being made at night.

Her post-Laird career was adventurous, and although it is known she went out South America, from this distance in time it is difficult to sort out the exact details of her ownership and service. She was sold in 1900, being then owned for a couple of years by a gentleman domiciled in San Francisco. By 1904 she was with the Colombian Government as PADILLA, reverting to IVY by 1905 when her owner hailed from Coquimbo in Chile. In 1906 IVY went to the Antofagasta Railway Company, who seem to have briefly reinstated the name PADILLA, but she then reverted to IVY. In 1912 she went to a third South American country, Peru, where she was renamed FENICE. On 9th April 1921 the ageing Londonderry-built steamer was wrecked on Lobos de Tierra islands.

BURNS BELFAST MAIL STEAMERS

ALLIGATOR (top)

Barclay, Curle and Co., Whiteinch; 1881, 932gt, 250 feet
C. 2-cyl. by Barclay, Curle and Co., Whiteinch

The iron screw steamer ALLIGATOR and her two sisters, DROMEDARY and GORILLA (the latter not illustrated, 929/1881), were built for the Glasgow-Belfast mail service. Burns won the contract for this service in 1849 by the simple expedient of offering to carry the mail free, and headed off a threatened rival service. However, soon after the entry into service of ALLIGATOR and her sisters, the contract was put on a proper commercial footing.

In 1907 the ALLIGATOR was sold to McDowall and Barbour of Piraeus, who already had the former BEAR and OWL, and was renamed ISMENE. After a long period of stability she was sold in 1927 and in just six years had three further owners and carried the names AFOVOS and RODOS. She was broken up in 1933.

ALLIGATOR was photographed from the Glasgow Sailor's Home, with Sloan's steamer MEDWAY (870/1886) beyond her. *[Donald McColl collection]*

DROMEDARY (bottom)

Barclay, Curle and Co., Whiteinch; 1881, 922gt, 250 feet
C. 2-cyl. by Barclay, Curle and Co., Whiteinch

DROMEDARY and her sisters were essentially enlargements of the WALRUS and MASTIFF of 1878, with some increase in passenger accommodation and more powerful engines to give them a service speed of 14 knots.

In contrast to her contemporaries, DROMEDARY went west rather than east when Burns sold her in 1909. New owners were the Reid Newfoundland Co. of St John's who renamed her INVERMORE. Her end came on 10th July 1914 when she was wrecked at Brigpoint, Labrador whilst on a voyage from St. John's to Labrador with provisions and fishery supplies. *[Glasgow University Archives, DC101/0204]*

THE LAST PADDLERS

COBRA (top)
Fairfield Shipbuilding and Engineering Co. Ltd., Govan; 1889, 817gt, 265 feet
Horizontal diagonal 2-cyl. by Fairfield Shipbuilding and Engineering Co. Ltd., Govan
In May 1860 Burns first tried to establish a daylight return service from Greenock to Belfast with the paddle steamer GIRAFFE (677/1860), which was intended to run at 20 knots. Partly because GIRAFFE could not sustain this speed on a daily basis, the service only lasted one summer. On the outbreak of the American Civil War in 1862 Burns was no doubt delighted to sell the GIRAFFE for use as a Confederate blockade runner.

In 1889 a renewed attempt was made to run a daily return service to Belfast, this time from Gourock, with another specially-designed paddler, the COBRA. But she too lasted just one season, after which she was returned to her builders. In 1890 Fairfields sold her to the Liverpool and Llandudno Steamship Co. Ltd., in which they had an interest, and she became ST. TUDNO. Sold again in 1891, she went to German owners for Hamburg-Heligoland sailings, reverting to the name COBRA. On this service she found stability, which was only disrupted by the First World War. In April 1919 she went as reparations to the French Government, but was never delivered and was broken up at Wismar in 1922. *[Peter Newall collection]*

ADDER (bottom and opposite)
Fairfield Shipbuilding and Engineering Co. Ltd., Govan; 1890, 771gt, 280 feet
C. 2-cyl. by Fairfield Shipbuilding and Engineering Co. Ltd., Govan
The ADDER was built to take the place of the COBRA on the Clyde-Belfast daylight service, re-opening sailings in July 1890. The Scottish terminal reverted to Greenock, but in 1893 Ardrossan was substituted when an agreement was reached with a railway company to provide a connection to Glasgow. ADDER's plain black funnels are reported to have been repainted buff with black tops on transfer to Ardrossan. In the accompanying photographs, however, her funnels are a similar colour to her boot topping, suggesting they were red with a black top.

With ADDER, the last of a long line of Burns' paddlers, the daylight Belfast service was at last successfully established and, after exceeding 20 knots on trials, she ran dependably until 1906 when she was sold. Her new owners took her all the way to Argentina and renamed her RIO DE LA PLATA. She was presumably rebuilt as a cargo steamer, as she was carrying general cargo from Buenos Aires to Santos when wrecked at Maldonado on Christmas Eve 1918. *[Below: National Library of Ireland; opposite: Glasgow University Archives, DC101/0002]*

HARE AND HOUND

HARE (top)
Barclay, Curle and Co. Ltd., Whiteinch; 1886, 614gt, 216 feet
T. 3-cyl. by Barclay, Curle and Co. Ltd., Whiteinch

HARE's modest claims to fame were being Burns' first steamer with triple expansion engines and the first to have electric lighting. She was indeed the electric HARE.

At various times she ran to Belfast from both Glasgow and and Ardrossan, and also relieved the MASTIFF on Londonderry sailings. This lack of permanence might suggest she was not altogether satisfactory in service, and she was sold in 1899 after only 13 years with Burns. New owners were Stewart and Lowen, for whom she sailed for the Dublin and Manchester Steamship Company between the ports in its title. She was carrying general cargo on such an eastbound sailing on 14th December 1917 when torpedoed by the German submarine U 62 east of the Kish Light Vessel, and sank with the loss of 12 lives. *[Glasgow University Archives DC101/1194]*

HOUND (bottom and opposite)
Fairfield Shipbuilding and Engineering Co. Ltd., Govan; 1893, 1,061gt, 250 feet
T. 3-cyl. by Fairfield Shipbuilding and Engineering Co. Ltd., Govan

HOUND definitely outran the smaller HARE, clocking up 32 years of Burns' sailings to Belfast, first from Ardrossan and later from Glasgow. She survived to swap Burns' plain black funnel for the former funnel of Laird, carried under Burns and Laird ownership.

In 1925 HOUND was sold to M.G.A. Manuelides Brothers of Piraeus as MARY M. In 1930 she passed to Hellenic Coast Lines Ltd., becoming LESBOS in 1933, and KORYTZA in 1942. She went to breakers in 1950. She is seen opposite with Burn's plain black funnel, and below in early Burns and Laird livery. *[Bottom: World Ship Photo Library collection; opposite: Glasgow University Archives]*

TWO DOGS
SPANIEL (1) (top and middle) and **CALORIC** (bottom)

A. and J. Inglis, Pointhouse; 1895, 942gt, 250 feet

T. 3-cyl. by A. and J. Inglis, Pointhouse

The sisters SPANIEL and POINTER were developments of the HARE and HOUND. Their fidded masts were evidently to reduce their overall height to allow transit of the Manchester Ship Canal, which opened the year SPANIEL was built. SPANIEL was placed on the Glasgow-Mersey service following the disagreement with MacIvers mentioned on page 8, running with Burns' MASTIFF and the CUMBRAE (916/1882) chartered from the Clyde Shipping Co. Ltd.

SPANIEL could be distinguished from her sister POINTER because she had a shorter steam pipe behind her funnel. The difference was attributable to SPANIEL's funnel needing to be lengthened after completion: in the upper, trials photograph her funnel is distinctly shorter than in the middle shot. SPANIEL's steam pipe was not lengthened to match the funnel, but POINTER enjoyed a full height funnel and steam pipe from the outset.

SPANIEL lost her passenger accommodation in 1921 and, as one of the first results of the Coast Lines' takeover, was transferred to the Belfast Steamship Co. Ltd. As CALORIC she ran as a cargo and cattle carrier, and was sold for breaking up at Dunston-on-Tyne in January 1932. *[Top: Glasgow University Archives DC101/1560]*

POINTER (1) (top) and **LAIRDSVALE** (middle and bottom)
A. and J. Inglis, Pointhouse; 1896, 1,183gt, 250 feet
T. 3-cyl. by A. and J. Inglis, Pointhouse
POINTER was used on Ardrossan-Belfast and Glasgow-Londonderry sailings, and she is seen leaving on one of the latter in the bottom photograph, after she had become LAIRDSVALE. The date is 15th July 1931, usually the time of Glasgow Fair Fortnight holidays, but her passenger numbers appear quite light. Note how a little white paint and white canvas dodgers alter her appearance from the upper photograph. LAIRDSVALE was approaching the end of her career when the 1931 photograph was taken, and in March 1933 she was sold to the Hughes Bolckow Shipbreaking Co. Ltd. at Blyth for breaking up.
[Top: World Ship Photo Library collection]

CARGO SHIPS

GROUSE (top)

Caird and Co. Ltd., Greenock; 1891, 410gt, 175 feet

T. 3-cyl. by Caird and Co. Ltd., Greenock

Burns' passenger and cargo ships of the 1890s had little enough superstructure, but in comparison with the pure cargo ships such as GROUSE it was capacious. In the case of GROUSE and her near-sister APE, cargo also included capacity for 80 cattle and 11 horses. They were hardly beauties, and nor were their names, but GROUSE has a very purposeful air in this classic shot in the Firth of Clyde.

GROUSE was transferred to the new Burns and Laird Lines Ltd. in 1922 but in the same year she was auctioned for just £855 to Grahamston Shipping Co. Ltd. of Glasgow and renamed KELVINDALE for a service from Glasgow and Greenock to Campbeltown, Stranraer and Preston. Coast Lines took over this service in November 1923 and in October KELVINDALE returned to Burns and Laird, but in June 1924 was transferred to Coast Lines and given the name DENBIGH COAST. In 1929 she moved to David MacBrayne, being renamed LOCHDUNVEGAN, and lasting with them until 1948 when she was broken up at Faslane by Metal Industries Ltd. *[Glasgow University Archives]*

APE (left)

Barclay, Curle and Co. Ltd., Whiteinch; 1898, 427gt, 175 feet

T. 3-cyl. by Barclay, Curle and Co. Ltd., Whiteinch

Seven years after GROUSE, Burns took delivery of a near-sister, APE, from Barclay, Curle for the Greenock-Belfast cargo service, which included weekly calls at Larne. This scene of her loading at Greenock shows cargo handling in pre-internal combustion engine days, with a steam crane, wooden railway wagons, a horse and cart, plus aching muscles and backs. In addition to her two derricks, APE has what appears to be a deck crane forward of her bridge, a fitting absent in GROUSE.

Despite being younger, APE was the first to go, replaced by the SABLE in 1912 and sold to Norwich owners. But it was not until 1918, and after further ownership in London, that she was renamed, becoming FETLAR of the North of Scotland, Orkney and Shetland Steam Navigation Co. Ltd. Her service with the North Company was woefully short, however, and on 13th April 1919 she struck Bunel Rocks in St. Malo Roads and sank.

LAIRD LINERS OF THE 1890s

OLIVE (top) and **LAIRDSBANK** (1) (bottom)

D. and W. Henderson, Meadowside; 1893, 1,047gt, 260 feet

T. 3-cyl. by D. and W. Henderson, Meadowside

OLIVE was the largest ship yet built for Laird Line, with accommodation for 100 saloon passengers and a massive 1,000 in steerage.

Most of them must have been on deck when, as LAIRDSBANK (lower photograph), she was leaving the Broomielaw for Londonderry in her final year with Burns and Laird. Much was made of the fact that she had fan ventilators for the convenience of transporting cattle, but no mention was made of the convenience of the passengers.

LAIRDSBANK was sold in 1930 to the North of Scotland, Orkney and Shetland Steam Navigation Co. Ltd. to replace their ST SUNNIVA (864/1887) and renamed ST. CATHERINE. She was scrapped at Rosyth in 1937. [Top: Glasgow University Archives DC101/0455]

SMALLER LAIRD LINERS OF THE 1890s

DAISY (2) (top)
Blackwood and Gordon, Port Glasgow; 1895, 419gt, 187 feet
T. 3-cyl. by Blackwood and Gordon, Port Glasgow
Altogether more modest than OLIVE, the DAISY had a unique profile in Laird's fleet, with a raised shelter deck extending almost to her stern. She was built for the Portrush trade, but also served Coleraine, and continued on this year-round service when the Portrush sailings were discontinued during the First World War. But Coleraine's River Bann had a notoriously difficult entrance and, when inward bound from Glasgow on 23rd February 1915, DAISY was caught by a heavy swell at Bannmouth and wrecked. *[Glasgow University Archives DC101/0188]*

FERN (2) (middle)
Ailsa Shipbuilding Co., Troon; 1899, 401gt, 180 feet
T. 3-cyl. by Dunsmuir and Jackson, Glasgow
Seen with the classic backdrop of a Clyde shipyard, FERN was, like DAISY and LILY, another modest steamer built to meet the traffic needs of the west of Ireland. Like DAISY, she came to a premature end, but in her case due to enemy action. On 22nd April 1918 she was five miles off the Kish Light Vessel when torpedoed and sunk by the German submarine U 194. Wartime had disrupted services, and at the time of her loss FERN was carrying general cargo from Dublin to Heysham.

LILY (bottom), **LAIRDSPOOL** (opposite top) and **LOCHGORM** (opposite bottom)
Blackwood and Gordon, Port Glasgow; 1896, 635gt, 191 feet
T. 3-cyl. by Blackwood and Gordon, Port Glasgow
After initial service between Ardrossan and Portrush, LILY became a fixture on the long haul from Glasgow to Westport, Sligo and Ballina in the west of Ireland: she must have had some testing times in the Atlantic swell. In 1936 Burns and Laird agreed to withdraw from this service in favour of the Sligo

Steam Navigation Co. Ltd, another Coast Lines subsidiary. LAIRDSPOOL, as she had become in 1929, was chartered for a time to the British and Irish Steam Packet Co. Ltd.: the top photograph opposite may show her in their funnel colours. In November 1936 she was first chartered, then acquired, by David MacBrayne, who gave her the name

LOCHGORM. She was used on services from Glasgow to the West Highlands, and in summer from Glasgow to Stornoway. She lasted until 1951 when she was broken up by Smith and Houston Ltd. at Port Glasgow, the town of her birth 55 years earlier.
[Bottom: Ambrose Greenway collection]

PASSENGERS AMIDSHIPS
MAGPIE (upper two) and **LAIRDSGROVE** (lower three)

A. and J. Inglis Ltd., Pointhouse; 1898, 1,280gt; 265 feet
T. 3-cyl. by A. and J. Inglis, Pointhouse

The evolution of Burns' steamers took a significant step forward with MAGPIE and VULTURE, whose passenger accommodation was placed amidships and a dining saloon placed in a deckhouse on the poop. Like SPANIEL and POINTER, they were given fidded masts so that topmasts could be lowered to navigate the Manchester Ship Canal if necessary.

MAGPIE was first used on Glasgow-Belfast sailings, but transferred to the Londonderry service when WOODCOCK arrived in 1906, being used on these latter sailings for much of her long life. In 1923 she was fitted with new boilers and the opportunity was taken to improve her accommodation. Some of the external changes are apparent in the third, post-1929 view of her as LAIRDSGROVE. She ceased carrying passsengers in 1939, and is seen alongside Anderston Quay in the bottom photograph with her passenger accommodation removed.

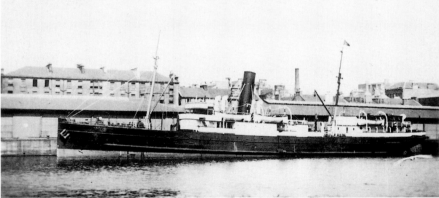

After 50 years on the Irish Sea LAIRDSGROVE was sold to Metal Industries Ltd. in 1948 and towed to Faslane for demolition (below). However, she had an extension of life when the breakers used her as an accommodation ship and she was not broken up until 1950. *[Top: Glasgow University Archives DC101/1342]*

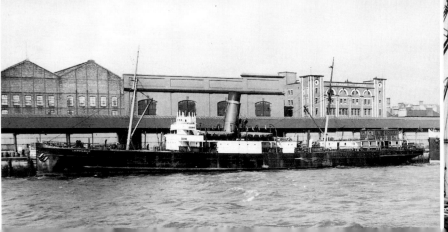

VULTURE (top), **LAIRDSROCK** (1) (middle) and **LOCHGARRY** (bottom)
A. and J. Inglis, Pointhouse; 1898, 1,280gt, 265 feet
T. 3-cyl. by A. and J. Inglis, Pointhouse

VULTURE was used mainly on Glasgow-Belfast and Ardrossan-Belfast sailings, except during the First World War when she operated from Aberdeen to Bergen. Otherwise her Burns and Laird career was similar to that of sister MAGPIE, also being taken in hand by D. and W. Henderson in 1924 for new boilers and upgraded accommodation. The top photograph shows her in this condition.

One wonders whether Burns gave any thought to marketing when naming their steamers: the name VULTURE was hardly likely to appeal to intending passengers. However, the individualistic animal nomenclature was preferable to the insipid made-up words used after May 1929, when VULTURE became LAIRDSROCK.

When the ROYAL SCOTSMAN and ROYAL ULSTERMAN were delivered in 1936, the Ardrossan-Belfast night sailings were discontinued, making LAIRDSROCK redundant. She was initially chartered to David MacBrayne Ltd., and in 1937 sold to the company as LOCHGARRY. For use on summer cruises she was considerably modified, as the bottom photograph shows, with extra accommodation and a new funnel. The Second World War ended her West Highland cruises, and LOCHGARRY was requisitioned by the Government, helping in the evacuation of Dunkirk and later operating between Scotland and Iceland. Sadly, on 21st January 1942, whilst on passage from Glasgow to Oban in ballast, LOCHGARRY struck a rock off Torr Head, County Antrim and foundered. *[Top J.B. MacGregor; bottom: G.E. Langmuir]*

TURBINES

VIPER (opposite and top) and **SNAEFELL** (bottom)

Fairfield Shipbuilding and Engineering Co. Ltd., Govan; 1906, 1,713gt, 315 feet
Three steam turbines by Fairfield Shipbuilding and Engineering Co. Ltd., Govan driving triple screws

Burns invested considerably in their Ardrossan-Belfast daylight service, and in 1906 this route saw the most splendid passenger steamer they had ordered so far, the turbine-driven VIPER. She replaced the paddler ADDER, and continued the tradition of snake names for fast steamers on the route: the coiled golden viper which decorated her forward bulwarks can just be discerned in the photograph opposite. Her Fairfield turbines gave her a speed of 22 knots, but it is salutary to note that her reciprocating-engined predecessor had managed 20 knots on trials.

The Ardrossan-Belfast daylight service was suspended during the First World War, but VIPER was kept busy on trooping voyages across the English Channel. She briefly returned to her old route in the summer of 1919, but the troubles in Ireland discouraged the tourists on which the service depended, and it was abandoned in July 1920. The surplus VIPER was sold to the Isle of Man Steam Packet Co. Ltd. who renamed her SNAEFELL.

SNAEFELL continued to be a frequent sight in Ardrossan, although she also took sailings to Douglas from Heysham and Liverpool. During the Second World War she maintained the Isle of Man's links with the mainland when most of her running mates were called up for war service. Evidently worn out, she was sold to Smith and Houston Ltd. in the autumn of 1945, but other work at their Port Glasgow yard meant that breaking up was not completed until early in 1949. *[Opposite: Ulster Museum]*

ARDROSSAN-BELFAST STEAMERS
WOODCOCK (top), **LAIRDSWOOD** (1) (middle) and **RENA** (bottom)
John Brown and Co. Ltd., Clydebank; 1906, 1,523gt, 270 feet
T. 3-cyl. by John Brown and Co. Ltd., Clydebank
Two months after the excitement of the delivery of VIPER in May 1906, two new ships arrived for the Ardrossan-Belfast night mail service, WOODCOCK and her sister PARTRIDGE being delivered on 2nd and 10th July 1906 respectively at a total cost of £100,000. Duckworth and Langmuir maintain that they were intended for the Glasgow-Belfast express service, but were not fast enough. Nevertheless, they were fine ships, representing an improvement over MAGPIE and VULTURE especially in terms of their steerage accommodation.

During the First World War both were employed as armed boarding steamers, being requisitioned in November 1914 and not released until 1920. WOODCOCK was renamed WOODNUT to avoid confusion with General Steam's similar-sized WOODCOCK (1,673/1906).

The photograph of LAIRDSWOOD, as she became in May 1929, depicts her in her last months with Burns and Laird, as she was sold to the Aberdeen Steam Navigation Co. Ltd. in November 1930 and renamed LOCHNAGAR.

In 1946 she began a new and rather different career. Sold to Panos Protopapas of Alexandria, she was put under the Panama flag as RENA and in 1948 and 1949 was employed between Europe and Australia carrying 360 emigrants - a far cry from her swift dashes across the Irish Sea. In the bottom photograph at Genoa on 25th March 1951 RENA still has her original fidded masts and steam cranes. Later that year she was renamed BLUE STAR, but on 26th April 1952 arrived at La Spezia for breaking up. *[Top: Ambrose Greenway collection; bottom: William Schell]*

PARTRIDGE (top) and **LAIRDSLOCH** (bottom)
John Brown and Co. Ltd., Clydebank; 1906, 1,523gt, 270 feet
T. 3-cyl. by John Brown and Co. Ltd., Clydebank

PARTRIDGE's saloon passenger figures were given as 436 in the accommodation aft, whilst midship steerage numbers were quoted as 697. With these numbers packed into a modest-sized ship, it is hardly surprising that photographs of them sailing, as in this case, show so many passengers massed on deck. There were also permanent fittings for 315 cattle and 4 horses, the presence of these beasts undoubtedly adding to the atmosphere on board.

When called up in the First World War PARTRIDGE initially became an armed boarding steamer, but later appears to have been employed as a transport between Malta and Marseilles, being renamed PARTRIDGE II in 1916.

PARTRIDGE was returned to her owners in 1920, and in later years was used, with WOODCOCK, largely on Dublin services. Late in 1936 LAIRDSLOCH, as she had become in 1929, made her way up to Dalmuir shipbreaking yard of W.H. Arnott, Young and Co. to be scrapped within sight of her birthplace.

THE DUKE LINE
DUKE OF ARGYLL (top)
Rankin and Blackmore, Greenock; 1873, 697gt, 250 feet
2-cyl. by R. Duncan and Co., Port Glasgow
On 1st May 1908, G. and J. Burns took over the business of the Dublin and Glasgow Sailing and Steam Packet Company and its four screw passenger steamers. This company bought its first steamer in 1836, and from 1869 names beginning 'Duke' were used, the company not unnaturally becoming known as the Duke Line. The iron DUKE OF ARGYLL was the final paddle steamer built for the company, and the last paddler on a regular night service from the Clyde: Burn's ADDER, which outlasted her slightly, was on a daylight service. DUKE OF ARGYLL went for breaking up at Dublin in November 1905, a few years before the company lost its independence.

GENERAL GORDON (upper middle) and DUKE OF GORDON (lower middle and bottom)
A. and J. Inglis, Pointhouse; 1885, 1,294gt, 230 feet
T. 3-cyl. by A. and J. Inglis, Pointhouse
Burns were determined to popularise the service between Dublin and the Clyde they had bought, and instituted a direct express cargo and passenger service between Glasgow and Dublin which left every Tuesday evening. The equivalent return sailing left Dublin on Thursday evening and called at Wemyss Bay where a train provided a fast connection to Glasgow. Two of the Duke Line vessels were almost new, so there was no urgency to replace them, and it was not until 1912 that Burns built a new ship for the Dublin route, the ERMINE.

The oldest of the Dublin and Glasgow ships taken over by Burns had been launched in April 1885 as GENERAL GORDON, the company's first screw steamer. To bring her into line with the other ships, she was renamed DUKE OF GORDON in February 1895, and at some point the superstructure was rebuilt as seen in the lower middle photograph. GENERAL GORDON is seen in the bottom photograph at Bristol on what is a charter to either William Sloan and Co. or the Bristol Steam Navigation Co. Ltd.

In 1908 the ownership of DUKE OF GORDON was transferred to the Burns Steamship Co. Ltd., a company newly formed to own the Dublin and Glasgow ships. DUKE OF GORDON was renamed WREN, being occasionally used on services other than to Dublin, including Londonderry and Liverpool. In 1914 she was bought by Administration des Navires à Vapeur Ottomane of Constantinople and renamed EUREUK, a name which was later rendered as YEYREUK. On 18th April 1920 she was wrecked at Amtchiros, about 90 miles into a voyage from Samsun to Constantinople. *[Upper middle: World Ship Photo Library collection; lower middle: Glasgow Transport Museum; bottom: George Scott collection]*

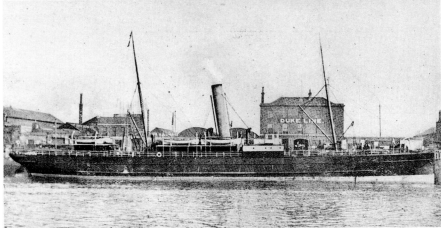

DUKE OF FIFE

Ailsa Shipbuilding Co., Troon; 1892, 753gt, 244 feet
T. 3-cyl. by Dunsmuir and Jackson, Glasgow

The Dublin and Glasgow company's second screw steamer was DUKE OF FIFE. The upper view shows her on trials and she is immaculate: the canvas covers on lifeboats are white, as are the sails closely brailed to the two masts. Her funnel is black, yellow being adopted by the Duke Line later in 1892.

The lower photograph shows her after she has undergone slight modification - note how the bridge has been raised - and she carries more white paint and a yellow funnel.

The DUKE OF FIFE became SPARROW in May 1908 when Burns acquired the company. No photographs of her have been found as SPARROW, however, probably because the Burns Steamship Co. Ltd. soon sold her, and in June 1910 she became ARCADIA of P. Pantaleon, Smyrna. She was sold to the Hellenic Coast Lines Co. Ltd. in 1927, and renamed CHIOS in 1933. During the axis attack on Greece, CHIOS was sunk by aircraft at Eretria near Chalkis on 18th April 1941. *[Top: Glasgow University Archives DC101/0212; bottom: Ambrose Greenway collection]*

THE DUKE LINE (continued)
DUKE OF ROTHESAY (top) and **LAIRDSFORD**
(1) (bottom and opposite)
*Caledon Shipbuilding and Engineering Co.
Ltd., Dundee; 1899, 1,226gt, 265 feet
T. 3-cyl. by Caledon Shipbuilding and
Engineering Co. Ltd., Dundee*
The DUKE OF ROTHESAY introduced to the
Glasgow and Dublin company the practice
of placing the first class accommodation
amidships. Previously, the saloon
passengers had been aft, and steerage
right forward. This arrangement had been
introduced to the Burns fleet the previous
year with MAGPIE.

The DUKE OF ROTHESAY is seen
under her original name above, and much
later in life as LAIRDSFORD. From 1908 until
1929 she ran as the PUMA, initially for the
Burns Steamship Co. Ltd. Count the
windows in the saloon. There are four,
matching the number of letters in her original
Burns' name. And there are five for her
near-sister, TIGER.

After spending all her life on the
Dublin service, LAIRDSFORD went to
breakers at Preston on 7th February 1934:
the final photograph shows her at T.W.
Ward's yard. *[Top: Glasgow University
Archives DC101/0209]*

THE DUKE LINE (continued)
DUKE OF MONTROSE (top), **LAIRDSFOREST** (bottom and opposite top) and **LADY LOUTH** (opposite bottom)

Caledon Shipbuilding and Engineering Co. Ltd., Dundee; 1906, 1,389gt, 275 feet
Q. 4-cyl. by Caledon Shipbuilding and Engineering Co. Ltd., Dundee

A modest enlargement of the DUKE OF ROTHESAY but with quadruple expansion engines, the DUKE OF MONTROSE was launched on 10th April 1906 for the Duke Line. In the top photograph she makes a superb sight, almost effortlessly cutting through the waters of the Firth of Clyde. Her capacity was impressive too: 530 cattle, 3 horses, 164 saloon passenger, and 996 steerage passengers. She became TIGER in 1908 to conform with Burns naming policy and continued to trade to and from Dublin.

After the First World War TIGER was the first steamer to provide West Highland cruises from Liverpool, cruises which were later taken over by the KILLARNEY (1,849/1893). Renamed LAIRDSFOREST in 1929, she was transferred to British and Irish Steam Packet Co. Ltd. in 1931 and renamed LADY LOUTH. Her passenger accommodation was removed and she became a cattle carrier, masts and funnel being cut down for the Manchester Ship Canal. Three years later, after a disastrous fire at Birkenhead, she was broken up at Port Glasgow by Smith and Houston. *[Top: Ambrose Greenway collection]*

THE LAST LAIRD LINERS

ROSE (4) (bottom) and **LAIRDSROSE** (top)
A. and J. Inglis, Pointhouse; 1902, 1,151gt, 251 feet
T. 3-cyl. by A. and J. Inglis, Pointhouse

It is hard to imagine that vessels like this regularly carried more than 800 passengers on an overnight cross-channel service: in the photographs of her leaving Glasgow for Londonderry there is hardly room enough for them on deck. Her unsophisticated but capacious passenger accommodation probably appealed to the Admiralty, who used ROSE during the First World War to provide a service from Taranto, Italy to Greece opposite the MAPLE.

When Burns and Laird renamed their ships in 1929 she became LAIRDSROSE, but continued to be referred to as the ROSE: the LAIRD prefix was invariably dropped by those familiar with the company's steamers. She was broken up in 1949 at Bo'ness on the Forth.

LAIRDSROSE is seen in the upper photograph leaving her Broomielaw berth for Londonderry, and passing Currie's distinctive SHETLAND (1,846/1921), which is probably laid up. Funnels were repainted red with black top in 1929, following the renamings, but that of LAIRDSROSE appears to have no black top.

HAZEL (top and middle) and **MONA** (bottom)
*Fairfield Shipbuilding and Engineering Co.
Ltd., Govan; 1907, 853gt, 261 feet
T. 8-cyl. by Fairfield Shipbuilding and
Engineering Co. Ltd., Govan driving twin
screws*

The Laird Line always seemed more conservative than its bigger rivals G. and J. Burns, adopting innovations later and generally using smaller ships. The HAZEL was a case in point. Built a year after Burns' VIPER, she was designed for the Ardrossan-Portrush service, where a high speed was necessary to allow one ship to complete a round voyage each day. Like VIPER she came from Fairfields, masterbuilders of fast passenger craft, but she was given reciprocating engines rather than turbines, and these needed eight cylinders to reach the required 19 knots. Limitations of Portrush harbour - whose small size is apparent from the middle photograph - restricted her length and depth, and with her high superstructure and tall funnel she gained an unenviable reputation as a lively ship in a seaway.

HAZEL's Portrush service was suspended on the outbreak of war in 1914, and Admiralty requisition as an armed boarding steamer followed in November. On her return from war in February 1919, Laird Line seemed reluctant to put her back on the Portrush route, possibly because tourism was much reduced by the troubles in Ireland. In 1919 she was sold to become the MONA of the Isle of Man Steam Packet Co. Ltd., who were shortly to acquire the VIPER from G. and J. Burns. MONA's Manx service was on secondary and overnight services. Sold for scrap in November 1938, she was broken up by Edgar Rees of Llanelly. *[Top: Ambrose Greenway collection; middle: Donald McColl collection]*

Arrival of Scotch Steamers, Portrush

THE LAST LAIRD LINERS (continued)

ROWAN

D. and W. Henderson and Co. Ltd., Meadowside; 1909, 1,103gt, 281 feet
T. 3-cyl. by D. and W. Henderson and Co. Ltd., Meadowside

The ROWAN was the Laird Line's largest and finest steamer, whose tall, raked and cowl-topped funnel gave an appearance which belied her relatively modest length. During the First World War ROWAN served like other Burns and Laird steamers as an armed boarding steamer (lower photograph). But she will always be remembered in connection with the ROWAN disaster, the worst to affect Burns or Laird.

ROWAN sailed from Glasgow on the evening of Saturday, 8th October 1921, and delayed her departure from Greenock to await the Southern Syncopated Orchestra, a jazz band taking passage to Dublin during a tour of British music halls. When approaching Corsewall Point, Wigtownshire, ROWAN ran into thick fog. Ahead were seen the lights of another ship, but although ROWAN turned to starboard her stern was struck by the inward-bound steamer, the United States Shipping Board's WEST CAMAK (5,881/1920). Orders were given to prepare to abandon ship, and passengers were issued with lifejackets. But the ROWAN had swung across the channel, and was struck amidships on her starboard side by the CLAN MALCOLM (5,994/1917) which was following her out of the Clyde. After this second impact, ROWAN sank quickly, her master Captain Brown and members of the jazz band being amongst the fatalities.

ROWAN was held to blame for the first collision because of her speed in fog and failure to sound her whistle. For the second collision she was held one third responsible because of her failure to sound her whistle as a vessel stopped in the water, a decision that seems harsh given the short time after the first collision, and Captain Brown's immediate concern for preserving lives, which helped save some 70 people. *[Top: Glasgow University Archives, courtesy Peter Moir; bottom: Ballast Trust]*

MAPLE (top) and **LAIRDSGLEN** (1) (bottom)
Ailsa Shipbuilding Co. Ltd., Troon; 1914,
1,294gt, 261 feet
T. 3-cyl. by Ailsa Shipbuilding Co. Ltd.,
Troon

Marking a return to more modest
dimensions and appearance after the
ROWAN, the MAPLE was launched in
February 1914 to replace the AZALEA,
which was withdrawn and sold when she
entered service. MAPLE is shown above in
what appears to be a trials photograph: the
dark base to her funnel and painted-out
name apparently being due to later
retouching. It was not long before she
went off to war, operating a Marseilles-
Taranto-Malta-Port Said-Alexandria
service.

Returning from war MAPLE went
back on the Glasgow-Londonderry route,
becoming LAIRDSGLEN in 1929 and
thereafter running with LAIRDSROSE and
LAIRDSGROVE. In 1932 the distinctive cowl
was removed from her funnel (as in the
bottom photograph) and a year later the
forward end of her accommodation was
rebuilt, so that she gained an observation
lounge and a new, enclosed bridge.

Although she remained in familiar
waters, the Second World War saw the
steamer in more danger than in the First.
On the evening of 1st December 1939
LAIRDSGLEN passed the Cumbraes Light
outward bound and switched off her
navigation lights, only to collide with
Sloan's FINDHORN (1,121/1903) which was
steaming with dimmed lights. The

FINDHORN had to be beached in Kilchattan
Bay. Although her owners claimed £12,000
from Burns and Laird, who counter-claimed
for £4,000, blame was eventually laid on the
FINDHORN for not keeping clear of

LAIRDSGLEN.

LAIRDSGLEN's end came in 1951
when she was sold to Smith and Houston
Ltd. for demolition at Port Glasgow.

LOST IN THE AEGEAN

REDBREAST (1) (top and opposite)
A. and J. Inglis Ltd., Pointhouse; 1908, 1,313gt, 267 feet
T. 3-cyl. by A. and J. Inglis Ltd., Pointhouse
REDBREAST was the last of the classic Burns ships with a modest superstructure and just two derricks to serve her cargo holds. Duckworth and Langmuir have it that she replaced ALLIGATOR on the Glasgow to Belfast station, but ALLIGATOR was actually sold a year earlier.

The photograph of REDBREAST on the right was taken at Mudros during the Dardanelles campaign, and also shows some of the great variety of warships and transports assembled for this ill-starred operation. Officially described as a commissioned fleet messenger, REDBREAST is probably operating a shuttle services to one of Gallipoli beaches, and one wonders how many of the tin-hatted soldiers lining her decks survived Turkish shells and bullets. On a more homely note, the ship's name can be seen spelt out on the wooden casing around the aft steering position.

REDBREAST is reported to have operated as a Q-ship for six months in 1916, but had reverted to her messenger role when the U-boats got their revenge. On 15th July 1917 she was on passage between Skyros and the Doro Channel in the Aegean when torpedoed and sunk by UC 38. *[Top: Peter Newall collection; opposite: Glasgow University Archives DC101/1490]*

ERMINE (bottom)
Fairfield Shipbuilding and Engineering Co. Ltd., Govan; 1912, 1,836gt, 311 feet
Two T. 4-cyl. by Fairfield Shipbuilding and Engineering Co. Ltd., Govan driving twin screws

ERMINE represented the peak of development of the passenger/cargo steamer under Burns' ownership, being both the biggest ship the company built and the largest short-sea ship running out of the Clyde. Nevertheless, and despite experience with VIPER, she was not given turbines but two sets of four-crank, four-cylinder triple-expansion engines which had to be specially balanced to reduce vibration. She looks much more modern than REDBREAST, but a touch of white paint would have done wonders to brighten up what appears an extremely dour colour scheme, at least in a black-and-white photograph, with dark varnished teak superstructure. Her enclosed wheelhouse was another innovation, and must have

been appreciated on her occasional cruises from the Clyde to Iceland.

A total of 170 first class passengers were berthed and fed on the promenade and hurricane decks, second class passengers having their facilities on the main deck. An unspecified number of third class passengers was also carried, with cattle right forward. This extensive accommodation obviously impressed the Admiralty, who requisitioned ERMINE as a commissioned fleet messenger in July 1915. She too went off to the eastern Mediterranean for the Gallipoli landings, and was as unlucky as REDBREAST. On 2nd August 1917 she was mined and sunk off Stavros, Gulf of Orphiani in the Aegean. *[Glasgow University Archives DC101/1141]*

THE LAST BURNS PASSENGER STEAMERS
MOORFOWL (top) and **LAIRDSMOOR** (1)
(middle upper and lower and opposite)
A. and J. Inglis Ltd., Pointhouse; 1919, 1,464gt, 265 feet
T. 3-cyl. A. and J. Inglis Ltd., Pointhouse
Although ordered by G. and J. Burns for their Belfast trade, a dispute with the builders led to this ship being launched as KILLARNEY for the City of Cork Steam Packet Co. Ltd., which had lost six ships during the First World War and were desperate for new tonnage. But in 1920, membership of Coast Lines Group meant a reorganisation of both fleets, and the ship came back to G. and J. Burns under her intended name MOORFOWL. This was another example of how little thought went into naming Burns' ships: how many passengers must have referred to her as 'more foul'? Renaming was, for once, an improvement and she became LAIRDSMOOR on 30th May 1929.

Externally a smaller version of the unfortunate ERMINE, MOORFOWL is shown in original condition in the top photograph on this page, with Burns and Laird's first funnel colours, but otherwise in Burns' drab scheme. She was extensively altered in 1926 when a new observation lounge was added and her upper deck was extended. The upper middle photograph and that opposite show LAIRDSMOOR in this later condition, and with extensive and welcome areas of white paint, which tend to make her look smaller. The shot opposite shows her approaching Finnieston vehicular ferry on 14th July 1933, bound for Dublin.

The third photograph on this page shows her in her final months, with the funnel colours adopted in 1936. On passage from Dublin to Greenock on 7th April 1937 LAIRDSMOOR was in collision with Shaw Savill's TARANAKI (8,448/1928) at 03.20 hours in dense fog off Black Head. She had 33 crew and 6 passengers on board, and TARANAKI rescued all passengers and crew with the exception of the master, Captain Campbell, and a fireman. *[Top: Glasgow Museum of Transport; middle lower: World Ship Photo Library]*

BURNS CARGO SHIPS 1906-1920
SETTER (1) (bottom)
Scott's Shipbuilding and Engineering Co. Ltd., Greenock; 1906, 993gt, 225 feet
T. 3-cyl. by Scott's Shipbuilding and Engineering Co. Ltd., Greenock
Having no passenger accommodation amidships, SETTER had a distinctly different profile from the rest of the Burns' fleet, but 'cargo ship' is not entirely accurate, as she did carry steerage passengers. With sister LURCHER, she was built for the Manchester trade, which explains her short masts, only slightly taller than her funnel. SETTER was on a routine voyage from Manchester to the Clyde with general cargo on 13th September 1918 when torpedoed by the German submarine UB 64 six miles off Corsewall Point. *[Glasgow Museum of Transport]*

BURNS CARGO SHIPS 1906-1920 (continued)
LURCHER (1) as **LADY MEATH** (top),
INNISCARRA (middle) and **MENAPIA**
(bottom)

*Scott's Shipbuilding and Engineering Co. Ltd.,
Greenock; 1906, 993gt, 225 feet
T. 3-cyl. by Scott's Shipbuilding and
Engineering Co. Ltd., Greenock*

As part of the rationalisation that followed
Coast Line's acquisition of G. and J. Burns
Ltd., LURCHER was transferred to the British
and Irish Steam Packet Co. Ltd. in 1920 to
become LADY MEATH, as seen here. A
further move to the City of Cork Steam Packet
Co. Ltd. followed in 1925, and she became
INNISCARRA. In 1935 she finally passed out
of Coast Lines orbit, becoming MENAPIA of
Wexford Steamships Ltd. Smith and Houston
Ltd. broke up this rather ungainly steamer at
Port Glasgow in July 1939. *[Middle: World
Ship Photo Library]*

SETTER (2) as **LADY KILDARE** (top) and
ULSTER CASTLE (middle and bottom)
*William Beardmore and Co. Ltd., Dalmuir;
1920, 1,217gt, 245 feet*
*T. 3-cyl. by William Beardmore and Co. Ltd.,
Dalmuir*

Twenty feet longer, but no prettier, a
replacement SETTER was delivered in May
1920, the name being changed from
WHIPPET. But in just three months she was
sold to the British and Irish Steam Packet Co.
Ltd. and renamed LADY KILDARE, as seen on
24th September 1930. In 1931 a further
transfer within what was now the Coast Lines
Group saw her become ULSTER CASTLE of
the Belfast Steamship Co. Ltd., as seen below
in the Mersey. The middle photograph may
show her running in Burns and Laird or
British and Irish colours. ULSTER CASTLE
was broken up by T.W. Ward Ltd. at Preston in
1950. *[Middle: A. Duncan]*

BURNS CARGO SHIPS 1906-1920 (continued)

SABLE (left)
A. and J. Inglis, Pointhouse; 1911, 687gt, 195 feet
T. 3-cyl. by A. and J. Inglis, Pointhouse
SABLE and her much later sister CONEY were singularly ugly ships, but could move any cargo, no matter how awkward. They were particularly useful in carrying steel plate and machinery from the Clyde to the shipyards in Belfast.

SABLE was renamed LAIRDSELM in the summer of 1929, but life under her new name was brief. On 21st December 1929 LAIRDSELM left Glasgow at 17.00 hours with 200 tons of diesel engine sections destined for Harland and Wolff Ltd. in Belfast. There were problems with the ship's trim after her cargo shifted, and she put in to Loch Ryan around 02.00 hours on 22nd December and went to anchor. Around 09.30 hours she rolled over and sank, but her crew managed to get clear and rowed over to Cairnryan. *[World Ship Photo Library]*

LAIRDSFERRY (bottom and opposite top)
Harland and Wolff Ltd., Govan; 1918, 697gt, 195 feet
T. 3-cyl. by A. and J. Inglis Ltd., Pointhouse
The massive, stumpy masts of these cargo ships are seen to good effect in this photo, which also gives an idea of the length of the forehold. The CONEY was renamed LAIRDSFERRY in 1929, and her usefulness meant that she lasted in the Burns and Laird fleet until 1952, when she went for scrapping by Smith and Houston Ltd. at Port Glasgow.

BROOM as ULSTER STAR (opposite bottom)
Ramage and Ferguson Ltd., Leith; 1904, 576gt, 186 feet
T. 3-cyl. by Ramage and Ferguson Ltd., Leith
BROOM was one of Laird Line's few secondhand acquisitions, bought in July 1915 presumably to strengthen a fleet depleted by wartime requisitions. Her original owners were the Aberdeen, Leith and Moray Firth Steam Shipping Co. Ltd., who named her JAMES CROMBIE after their manager. She briefly passed through the ownership of Langlands of Glasgow before coming to Laird.

In 1922 Coast Lines decided BROOM was better employed by the City of Cork Steam Packet Co. Ltd., for whom she became LISMORE. Her fifth and final owners were the Belfast Steamship Co. Ltd., by whom this modest cargo steamer was dubbed DYNAMIC in 1923. When they, like Burns and Laird, succumbed to a corporate renaming scheme, DYNAMIC became ULSTER STAR in 1931 as seen opposite. She survived the Second World War, arriving at Troon on 17th February 1949 to be broken up by the West of Scotland Shipbreaking Co. Ltd.

OLDER AYR SHIPS
LAIRDSHEATHER (top)
Archibald MacMillan and Son, Dumbarton; 1889, 515gt, 190 feet
T. 3-cyl. by Kincaid and Co., Greenock

The Ayr Steam Shipping Co. Ltd., acquired by Lairds in 1908 but allowed to retain its identity until 1921, dated from around 1875, and operated passenger and cargo services from Ayr to Larne, Belfast and Campbeltown, and a cargo service from Glasgow to Barrow-in-Furness. Many of the company's cargoes were connected with the iron and steel industry of Ayrshire. The original managers were P. Barr and Co. and from 1883 David Rowan, better known as a Glasgow engine builder. About 1890 managers became Rowan and Bain.

The Ayr company bought most of its vessels secondhand, and some were seriously old. Two remained to be absorbed by the Laird Line Ltd in 1921, but only one survived to take a Burns and Laird corporate name

Completed as SPINDRIFT for C.F. Leach, London, she was acquired by the Ayr company in 1899 and given the local name TURNBERRY. Throughout acquisition and absorbtion by Laird, and renaming LAIRDSHEATHER by Burns and Laird, she is said to have remained steadfastly on the Ayr-Belfast service. The photograph shows her in the Mersey, however, and this may date it to the very end of her career. With reorganisation of the Ardrossan and Ayr-Belfast service following the arrival of the LAIRDSCREST and LAIRDSWOOD in 1936,

LAIRSDHEATHER became the spare vessel for a few months before being sold in March 1937 to T.W. Ward Ltd. for breaking up at Barrow-in-Furness.

DUNURE (bottom)
D. and W. Henderson, Meadowside; 1878, 748gt, 217 feet
C. 2-cyl. by D. and W. Henderson, Meadowside

The other Ayr Steam vessel to be absorbed into the Laird Line fleet was the DUNURE, 18 years after she had been sold by Laird as CEDAR. Ayr Steam Shipping Co. Ltd. bought her in 1906 and renamed her DUNURE to fill the vacancy left when their CARRICK (607/1885) was lost off Ailsa Craig after collision with DUKE OF GORDON in May 1906. In 1922 DUNURE came back into the Laird Line fleet and regained the old funnel of white base, red and black top. In February 1924 the company finally disposed of her, selling her to Ph. Kavounides of Piraeus who renamed her NICOLAOS KAVOUNIDES, then BOSPHOROS, and finally EXPRESS. In 1928 she was sold to Alex Yannoulatos, and carried the names ZEPHIROS and SPETSAI before going to breakers at Savona, Italy in 1937. *[Donald McColl collection]*

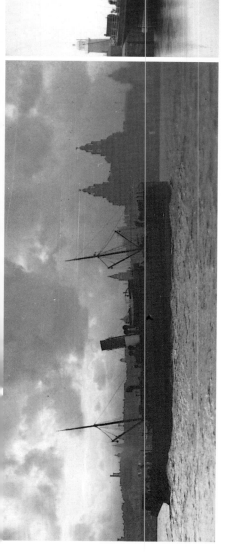

REPLACEMENT AYR SHIPS

CAIRNSMORE (top left) and **LADY KERRY** (bottom left)
Harland and Wolff Ltd., Belfast; 1886, 877gt, 236 feet
Two T. 3-cyl. by Harland and Wolff Ltd., Belfast driving twin screws

When Laird Line were faced with the problem of providing fresh ships for the routes formerly operated by Ayr Steam Shipping Co. Ltd., their new owners, Coast Lines, came to the rescue by transferring two vessels from other subsidiaries. The two sisters, COMIC and

LOGIC, which arrived in September 1921 from the Belfast Steamship Co. Ltd. were neither new nor fast, having been built around a quarter century earlier for the distinctly secondary Liverpool-Londonderry service, but passengers using the Ayr-Belfast and Larne sailings were used to nothing better. A nice touch was giving the ships local names in the Ayr company's tradition, the COMIC benefiting from the grander name of CAIRNSMORE, taken from the highest hill in Galloway, Cairnsmore of Fleet.

CAIRNSMORE escaped the renamings of May 1929, moving on to the British and Irish Steam

Packet Co. Ltd, Dublin in that year, her value now being a mere £2,000. She was now a grand old lady and was suitably named, in British and Irish style, LADY KERRY. She was broken up by T.W. Ward Ltd. at Preston in 1934. [Both: World Ship Photo Library collection]

CULZEAN (top right) and **LADY CARLOW** (bottom right)
Barclay, Curle and Co. Ltd., Whiteinch; 1898, 863gt, 236 feet
Two T. 3-cyl. by Barclay, Curle and Co. Ltd., Whiteinch driving twin screws

LOGIC was a near-sister of COMIC, and also spent much of her early career on the Liverpool-Londonderry service, which was closed when the two ships were transferred to Laird Line. In Laird's ownership LOGIC became CULZEAN, named after the home of the Marquis of Ailsa, Culzean Castle.

The two ships' careers proceeded in parallel, and CULZEAN was transferred with CAIRNSMORE to the British and Irish fleet in 1929, becoming LADY CARLOW, also being valued at the £2,000 she was worth as scrap. She arrived at Port Glasgow in May 1936 to be broken up by Smith and Co..

CLYDE-MERSEY CARGO SHIPS
REDBREAST (2) as **SUTHERLAND COAST** (top) and **LAIRDSBROOK** (bottom)

Harland and Wolff Ltd., Glasgow; 1921, 760gt, 200 feet

T. 3-cyl. by A. and J. Inglis Ltd., Pointhouse

One of the first positive outcomes of the Coast Lines takeover was the building of four new cargo steamers for the trade between Glasgow and Liverpool and Manchester. Not surprisingly, the order for these four distinctive, if ungainly, ships went to Harland and Wolff Ltd., who were financially associated with Coast Lines through Lord Kylsant, who controlled both. The orders were shared between Harland and Wolff's Govan yard and the Pointhouse yard of A. and J. Inglis Ltd., which the Belfast-based company owned.

The Clyde-Mersey services were now operated under the title Burns-Langland, the latter half referring to Matthew Langlands and Co., an old-established Glasgow coasting company who were acquired by Coast Lines late in 1919. The name PRINCESS CAROLINE was originally chosen for the first of the quartet, a Langlands' name, but in March 1920 it was decided that Langlands were not to continue in existence as shipowners and their vessels were all registered in the ownership of Coast Lines Ltd. with COAST names. However, the PRINCESS CAROLINE was launched in October 1920 as REDBREAST for G. and J. Burns Ltd. Changes of name, ownership and trading titles were to be a continuing part of the lives of REDBREAST and her sisters.

In 1925 the Clyde-Mersey services were transferred from Burns and Laird Lines Ltd. to Coast Lines Ltd., and with it the ships built for this service, REDBREAST becoming SUTHERLAND COAST. In 1930, however, she came back to the Burns and Laird fleet as LAIRDSBROOK to replace the LAIRDSELM which had rolled over when her cargo shifted in Loch Ryan in December 1929. LAIRDSBROOK lasted until 1960, arriving at Passage West, Cork on 11th March to be broken up by Haulbowline Industries Ltd. *[Bottom: World Ship Photo Library]*

GORILLA (2) as KINSALE (top) and **CAMBRIAN COAST** (bottom)
Harland and Wolff Ltd., Govan; 1921, 758gt, 200 feet
T. 3-cyl. by A. and J. Inglis Ltd., Pointhouse
Plans for GORILLA show that she was originally to be a single-decker, with masts at the break of forecastle and poop. REDBREAST was probably built to this design, too. However, at some stage both were converted to shelter deckers, with the space between forecastle and poop decked in and the masts altered, which helps account for their ungainly appearance. Another change was that GORILLA was intended to be PRINCESS DAGMAR, but was launched late in December 1920 with the rather less attractive name.

Although the ship had a long and useful life, it almost ended after 18 months when GORILLA was sunk near Cork on 10th August 1922 during the troubles surrounding Irish independence. When raised, she was reconditioned in Glasgow by her builders.

In 1925 GORILLA began wandering around the Coast Lines Group, becoming first CUMBERLAND COAST, then KINSALE for the City of Cork Steam Packet Co. Ltd. in 1929, back to Coast Lines Ltd. in 1933 but this time as CAMBRIAN COAST, then on to the Belfast Steamship Co. Ltd. in 1947 as ULSTER MERCHANT. On 8th October 1954 she arrived at Newport, Monmouthshire to be broken up by John Cashmore Ltd. *[Top: A. Duncan]*

CLYDE-MERSEY CARGO SHIPS (continued)

LURCHER (2) (top left), **SCOTTISH COAST** (top right), **ULSTER COAST** (bottom left) and **AHERN TRADER** (bottom right)
A. and J. Inglis Ltd., Pointhouse; 1922, 774gt, 201 feet
T. 3-cyl. by A. and J. Inglis Ltd., Pointhouse

In the deteriorating trading conditions following the First World War, Coast Lines told Harland and Wolff to suspend work on the second pair of cargo ships, both building at Pointhouse. Somewhat to the relief of the builders, who were teetering on the brink of insolvency, work recommenced in 1922, and what was intended to have been the SCOTTISH COAST was launched as LURCHER in September.

After just three years with what had now become Burns and Laird Lines Ltd., LURCHER was transferred back to Coast Lines Ltd. and became SCOTTISH COAST. In 1938 she moved to Belfast Steamship Co. Ltd. as their ULSTER COAST. She was the only one of the quartet to be sold outside the Coast Lines Group and the only one lost. In 1954 she crossed the Atlantic to become the AHERN TRADER of the Ahern Shipping Co. Ltd. of Montreal. On 10th January 1960 whilst carrying a cargo of hay she went ashore at the delightfully-named Muddy Hole in Gander Bay, Newfoundland after she had broken adrift during a snowstorm and soon broke up.

SPANIEL (2) (top), **AYRSHIRE COAST** (middle) and **ULSTER MARINER** (bottom)

A. and J. Inglis Ltd., Pointhouse; 1922, 773gt, 201 feet

T. 3-cyl. by A. and J. Inglis Ltd., Pointhouse

Both LURCHER and AYRSHIRE COAST were completed as shelter deckers. Again there was a change of mind about the latter's name: it was originally intended to be LADY OLIVE, suggesting ownership by the British and Irish Steam Packet Co. Ltd., but in August 1922 she was launched as AYRSHIRE COAST, and in October delivered to Coast Lines Ltd. Within a year she moved to Burns and Laird as SPANIEL, only to revert to AYRSHIRE COAST in 1925, remaining throughout on the Clyde-Mersey services.

After a remarkable 22 years without a change of name, in 1947 she became the ULSTER MARINER of the Belfast Steamship Co. Ltd. Her last voyage ended on 22nd July 1955 when she arrived at Passage West to be broken up by Haulbowline Industries Ltd. *[Bottom: A. Duncan]*

SETTER (2) as PRINCESS LOUISE
D. and W. Henderson and Co., Meadowside, Glasgow; 1888, 868gt, 226 feet T. 3-cyl. by D. and W. Henderson, Meadowside, Glasgow 1908: T. 3-cyl. by Clyde Shipbuilding and

Engineering Co. Ltd., Port Glasgow
As part of the rationalisation of the Clyde-Mersey trade in 1920, Langland's PRINCESS LOUISE - which had been running between Glasgow, Liverpool and Manchester (as in this photograph) since

1901 - was taken over by Coast Lines Ltd. and renamed CLYDE COAST. A change of heart saw her transferred to Burns and Laird in 1923 to become SETTER, remaining on the Burns-Langlands' service to the Mersey. On the move twice in 1925 she

went back to Coast Lines again as CLYDE COAST and later that year to City of Cork Steam Packet Co. Ltd. as MACROOM. She was broken up at Port Glasgow in 1929.

IRISH SHIPS TRANSFERRED

LADY LONGFORD (top) and **LAIRDSHILL** (bottom)

Ardrossan Drydock and Shipbuilding Co. Ltd., Ardrossan; 1921, 1,776gt, 285 feet
T. 3-cyl. by J. G. Kincaid and Co. Ltd., Greenock

The 1920s saw no additions to the Burns and Laird passenger fleet, despite losses of REDBREAST and ERMINE during the war, the sale of HAZEL and VIPER soon afterwards, and the sinking of ROWAN in 1921. With some of its newest, biggest and fastest ships gone, the company's services were maintained by vessels which, in several cases, had been built in the previous century. Some improvement came in 1930, with the transfer of three relatively new ships plus one veteran from other Irish Sea services.

The three vessels described, not particularly frankly, as 'luxurious vessels of the latest oil-burning type', became available as a result of the delivery to the Belfast Steamship Co. Ltd. of three new motorships for their Liverpool-Belfast service: ULSTER MONARCH, ULSTER QUEEN and ULSTER PRINCE. They allowed the transfer of HEROIC, PATRIOTIC and GRAPHIC to the British and Irish Steam Packet Co. Ltd., and the latter company in turn moved three steamers to Burns and Laird.

ARDMORE had been built for the Fishguard service of the City of Cork Steam Packet Co. Ltd. but was transferred to the British and Irish Steam Packet Co. Ltd. in 1923 to become LADY LONGFORD. On coming to Burns and Laird's Glasgow-Dublin service she was renamed LAIRDSHILL. Six years later she went back to British and Irish Steam Packet Co. Ltd., reverted to the name LADY LONGFORD, and had her masts shortened and her funnel cut at a rakish angle.

Following the sinking of LAIRDSMOOR, the steamer returned to Burns and Laird in 1937 as LAIRDSHILL. On 16th September 1939 she took the last Dublin service before the route's closure for the duration of the Second World War. Service resumed in June 1946, and LAIRDSHILL lasted until 1957, arriving at Dublin on 9th July to be broken up by the Hammond Lane Foundry Ltd.

IRISH SHIPS TRANSFERRED (continued)

LADY LOUTH (top) and **LAIRDSBURN** (1) (bottom)

Ardrossan Drydock and Shipbuilding Co. Ltd., Ardrossan; 1923, 1,896gt, 287 feet

T. 3-cyl. by J. G. Kincaid and Co. Ltd., Greenock

Built as LADY LOUTH for the British and Irish Steam Packet Co. Ltd., in 1930 she became LAIRDSBURN for the Glasgow-Belfast overnight service. With her near sister, LAIRDSCASTLE, she remained on the route until the arrival of the ROYAL SCOTSMAN and ROYAL ULSTERMAN in 1936, after which they were transferred to the Glasgow-Dublin route. LAIRDSBURN lasted until 1953, when she was broken up at Port Glasgow.

In the lower photograph LAIRDSBURN is seen approaching Merklands Lairage on her morning arrival with cattle from Dublin. Passengers could disembark here as customs facilities were available, or they could remain on board for a further two hours while she made her way up to Anderston Quay.

LADY LIMERICK (top) and **LAIRDSCASTLE** (1) (bottom)

Ardrossan Drydock and Shipbuilding Co. Ltd., Ardrossan; 1924, 1,945gt, 287 feet
T. 3-cyl. J. G. Kincaid and Co. Ltd., Greenock

LAIRDSCASTLE, previously LADY LIMERICK of the British and Irish Steam Packet Co. Ltd., was lost during the Second World War, although - like LAIRDSGLEN - a victim of the reduced lighting of ships in wartime rather than direct enemy action. On 4th September 1940, whilst on passage from Glasgow to Belfast, she was in collision with Reardon Smith's VERNON CITY (4,748/1929) in fog between the Mull of Kintyre and Ailsa Craig, and sank after three hours. Fortunately, the sea was calm and her 72 passengers and 29 crew got away in the lifeboats to be rescued by a Royal Navy destroyer.

The top photograph, although beautifully crisp, has had the funnel colours retouched. It is almost certainly a trials shot: note the stem jack, the clutch of officers and others on the lower bridge, and her generally pristine condition. Although no name is visible on the bow, it almost certainly shows the ship as LADY LIMERICK. In the lower photograph, which also shows the dome of the Clyde Navigation Trust headquarters in Robertson Street, LAIRDSCASTLE is ready to depart from the Broomielaw for Belfast.

IRISH SHIPS TRANSFERRED (continued)

LAIRDSBEN (right)

Harland and Wolff Ltd., Belfast; 1893, 652gt, 219 feet

Two T. 3-cyl. by Harland and Wolff Ltd., Belfast driving twin screws

Older than many of Burns and Laird's own steamers, LAIRDSBEN had already known three owners when she was transferred in 1932. Launched as MYSTIC for Belfast Steamship Co. Ltd. she remained with them for 17 years before becoming CARRICKFERGUS of the City of Dublin Steam Packet Co. Ltd. in 1910. In 1917 she passed to Sligo Steam Navigation Co. Ltd. without change of name. LAIRDSBEN replaced LAIRDSBANK, carrying cargo and cattle between Londonderry and Heysham, with occasional sailings from Ayr. She was sold to Smith and Co. in 1936 for breaking up at Port Glasgow. [G.E. Langmuir, courtesy World Ship Photo Library collection]

ARDROSSAN-BELFAST REVIVED

RIVIERA (below) and **LAIRDS ISLE** (opposite)

Wm. Denny and Brothers Ltd., Dumbarton; 1911, 1,783gt, 316 feet

Three steam turbines by Wm. Denny and Brothers Ltd., Dumbarton driving triple screws

After a rather unhappy decade, the 1930s saw Burns and Laird's fortunes revive. First came the more modern ships for their major services, and then a successful attempt to revive the Ardrossan-Belfast daylight sailings, which needed a fast ship if tourists were to be allowed a significant time ashore. Late in 1932 the company bought the RIVIERA from the Southern Railway Company for a modest £4,100. She had been built for the South Eastern and Chatham Railway Company's Folkestone to Boulogne

service, and was reputed to be capable of 23 knots. LAIRDS ISLE, as she became after overhaul and conversion to oil burning, was the flyer in the fleet but produced great volumes of smoke to attain top speed, as testified by the bottom photograph taken leaving Ardrossan on 9th July 1951.

RIVIERA had been to war in 1914-18 as a seaplane carrier, and during the Second World War LAIRDS ISLE served her time as an armed boarding vessel, and later as a tender to a torpedo school. Finally, she was converted to an infantry landing ship for the Normandy landings. After 46 years' work, which included ten years' war service, LAIRDS ISLE retired to Albert Harbour, Greenock in 1957, and moved to Troon on 9th October 1957 to be broken up by the West of Scotland Shipbreaking Co. Ltd. *[This page top: B.L. Devenish-Meares; middle: Clyde River Steamer Club 7206, Donald McColl collection; bottom: Michael Crowdy, World Ship Photo Library]*

THE FIRST MOTOR LINERS
ROYAL SCOTSMAN (opposite top and bottom)
ROYAL ULSTERMAN (opposite top)

The ROYAL SCOTSMAN and ROYAL ULSTERMAN were entirely different from any previous Burns or Laird ships, being developments of the three ULSTER MONARCH class ships built in 1930 for the Belfast Steamship Co. Ltd. The pair were photographed on the ways on 6th March 1936, the ROYAL SCOTSMAN to the right still to receive her masts (opposite top). The latter was launched on 11th March 1936, a day after her sister (opposite bottom).

The engines for ROYAL ULSTERMAN were photographed (top) on their way to the fitting out berth on 30th April 1936. The self-propelled steam crane handling the bogie trolleys on which they sit contrasts with the high technology of these airless-injection diesels, developed by Frederick Rebbeck and C.C. Pounder of Harland and Wolff in collaboration with Burmeister and Wain of Copenhagen. Those who prefer steam may be interested to know that the crane was built by Taylor and Hubbard of Leicester, a company which built over 1,800 similar machines for railway and industrial use.

In contrast with the industrial scene above is the lounge of the ROYAL SCOTSMAN (right) with its portrait of Edward VIII.
[All: Ulster Folk and Transport Museum: 7828. 7847; 7966; 3879]

THE FIRST MOTOR LINERS
(continued)
ROYAL ULSTERMAN (opposite and top),
CAMMELL LAIRD (middle) and **SOUNION**
(bottom)

Harland and Wolff Ltd., Belfast; 1936, 3,288gt, 339 feet
Two 8 cyl. 2SCSA oil engines by Harland and Wolff Ltd., Belfast driving twin screws

The new ships represented a dramatic improvement in passenger facilities, especially in third class, where 110 souls could enjoy two-berth cabins, and their own restaurant, smoke room and lounge. The names were also a departure from tradition, although ROYAL ULSTERMAN was originally intended to be LAIRD OF ULSTER and ROYAL SCOTSMAN the LAIRD OF SCOTIA. A nice touch was registering the former in Belfast.

Both ships provided sterling service under both the red and the white ensign during the Second World War and were involved in most of the seaborne landings as landing ships, infantry or commando ships. From November 1942 to March 1943 they transported thousands of troops from the big troopships to smaller ports along the North African coast.

After the war they returned to the Glasgow-Belfast overnight service where they remained until 1967. During the 1950s and 1960s they regularly carried 30 passengers' cars, a cargo which had not been planned for, and had to be loaded by crane.

In 1968 ROYAL ULSTERMAN was sold to Cammell Laird and Co. (Shipbuilders and Engineers) Ltd. and renamed CAMMELL LAIRD to serve as an accommodation ship in their Birkenhead shipyard. In 1970 Greek owners put her back into service as the Cyprus-registered SOUNION. But a ship that had survived active service in the Mediterranean 30 years earlier now

became a victim of a war-like act, and she sank on 3rd March 1973 in Beirut as a result of an explosive device. She was refloated in April 1973 and in September arrived at Perama, Greece to be broken up. *[Bottom: Jim McFaul]*

THE FIRST MOTOR LINERS
(continued)
ROYAL SCOTSMAN (opposite and top) and
APOLLO (bottom)
Harland and Wolff Ltd., Belfast; 1936, 3,288gt, 339 feet
Two 8-cyl. 2SCSA oil engines by Harland and Wolff Ltd., Belfast driving twin screws
The only external difference between the ROYAL ULSTERMAN and the ROYAL SCOTSMAN was the weather vanes: that on the latter's mainmast was in the shape of a thistle, whilst her sister carried hers in the shape of a shamrock on the foremast. Unfortunately, the weather vane is obscured in the trials photograph on 11th June 1936 (opposite top), and ROYAL SCOTSMAN has had her mainmast removed between the two wartime shots, taken on 12th August 1942 (opposite bottom) and in 1943 (top)

When withdrawn in 1967 ROYAL SCOTSMAN was sold to Ron Hubbard of Scientology fame, who renamed her first ROYAL SCOTMAN (sic) and later APOLLO. She finished her days at Brownsville, Texas where, after proposals were made to turn her into a floating restaurant, and renaming ARCTIC STAR, she suffered one of the most bizarre accidents ever to send a ship to the breakers: a collision with seven runaway railway boxcars on 17th September 1980. She was broken up at Brownsville in 1984.
[Opposite top: Ulster Folk and Transport Museum 7997; this page top: Peter Newall collection]

NEW CARGO SHIPS

LAIRDSWOOD (2) (top) and **ULSTER SPORTSMAN** (middle)

Harland and Wolff Ltd., Belfast; 1936, 789gt, 229 feet

Two 5-cyl. 2SCSA oil engines by Harland and Wolff Ltd., Belfast driving twin screws

The ROYAL SCOTSMAN and ROYAL ULSTERMAN offered increased accommodation and allowed the overnight Ardrossan-Belfast service to be withdrawn. In its place a new triangular cargo service, Ayr-Ardrossan-Belfast, was introduced. This service required only two ships, but the opportunity was taken to build three sisters with the third vessel intended for the Heysham to Londonderry service.

LAIRDSWOOD was the first of the cargo ships to be delivered, and is seen above on trials on 12th August. She was remarkably little changed over the years, as is apparent from the middle photograph of her in the Mersey as ULSTER SPORTSMAN after transfer to the Belfast Steamship Co. Ltd. in 1959.

In 1966, after a creditable 30 years with the Coast Lines Group, she was sold to become TRANSRODOPI IV, then spending two years in Bulgarian ownership as ALNILAM. She was broken up in Spain during 1970. *[Top: Ulster Folk and Transport Museum 8028]*

LAIRDSCREST (bottom)

Harland and Wolff Ltd., Belfast; 1936, 789gt, 229 feet

Two 5-cyl. 2SCSA oil engines by Harland and Wolff Ltd., Belfast driving twin screws

For livestock and cargo ships, these three sisters were well equipped. Their diesels, of the airless-injection type developed by the builders in conjunction with Burmeister and Wain, drove them at 13.5 knots, and their twin screws would ensure excellent manoueverability. Space for around 300 cattle or horses, or many more sheep, was mechanically ventilated. LAIRDSCREST was launched on 6th August 1936, and joined LAIRDSWOOD to inaugurate the Ayr-Ardrossan-Belfast service in September.

LAIRDSCREST kept her name until 1968, and in later life could be distinguished from her sisters by a rather ugly lattice mast to carry her radar scanner. Life after Burns and Laird comprised a ten-year period

under the Panama flag as SAN MARCO and later KRONOS. She was broken up in 1978. [A. Duncan]

LAIRDSBANK (2) (top and middle) and **GLANMIRE** (bottom)
Harland and Wolff Ltd., Belfast; 1936, 789gt, 229 feet
Two 5-cyl. 2SCSA oil engines by Harland and Wolff Ltd., Belfast driving twin screws
Launched on 3rd September 1936, the third sister, LAIRDSBANK, was built to operate between Heysham to Londonderry. Early in her career she had what could have been a fatal accident when she ran ashore at Barncorkrie, a few miles north of the Mull of Galloway, in dense fog in the early hours of 6th April 1937 while on passage from Londonderry to Heysham with 200 cattle and 200 pigs (middle photograph). After an unsuccessful attempt to take her off at high water at 06.30 hours, the Portpatrick lifeboat stood by and eventually took off seven cattlemen, two of whom were on board the ENDA two years earlier when she was lost in approximately the same position. Clyde Shipping's tug FLYING FALCON (283/1934) pulled her off later that day and LAIRDSBANK made her own way to Ayr to land the livestock. She was to be moved to the Ailsa yard at Troon for attention to her holed bow and damaged underwater plating. The very next day in the continuing fog LAIRDSMOOR was in collision with Shaw Savill's TARANAKI and sank off Black Head, Wigtonshire (see page 45).

In 1963 LAIRDSBANK went as GLANMIRE to the British and Irish Steam Packet Co. Ltd. for their Cork service. She was broken up at Dalmuir in 1969, the first of the three sisters to go to the breakers.

THE LAST SLIGO STEAMER
SLIGO (top), **LAIRDSDALE** (middle) and
ULSTER DROVER (bottom)
*Dublin Dockyard Co. (Vickers (Ireland) Ltd).,
Dublin; 1930, 891gt, 230 feet*
*T. 3-cyl. by Mackie and Baxter Ltd., Glasgow
driving twin screws*
Almost unnoticed in the excitement of the
arrival of the two ROYALs, in 1936 the
company took over the last ship belonging to
Sligo Steam Navigation Co. Ltd., the
eponymous SLIGO, which became the
LAIRDSDALE. She continued her association
with the port of Sligo until 1954 when she was
transferred to the Belfast Steam Ship Co. Ltd.
to become their ULSTER DROVER. She
continued to make occasional extra cattle
runs to Glasgow under this name, until
broken up by the West of Scotland
Shipbreaking Co. Ltd. at Troon, where she
arrived on 9th November 1959. *[Bottom: A.
Duncan]*

FIRST WORLD WAR STANDARDS
WESTERN COAST (top), **MEATH** (middle), and **LAIRDSCASTLE** (2) (bottom)

Caledon Shipbuilding and Engineering Co. Ltd., Dundee; 1919, 1,434gt, 271 feet
T. 3-cyl. by Caledon Shipbuilding and Engineering Co. Ltd., Dundee

The complexity of Coast Lines' internal transfers becomes apparent from considering the careers of the First World War standard ships which the group bought in its early years, three of which passed through Burns and Laird ownership.

WESTERN COAST was launched as WAR LEVEN, becoming LIMOGES of James Moss and Co., Liverpool, before joining the fleet of Coast Lines in 1922. She was transferred to Burns and Laird in 1941, but remained WESTERN COAST because wartime restrictions did not allow a change to her intended name, LAIRDSVALE. In 1946 she was given the British and Irish name MEATH whilst still in Burns and Laird's ownership. In 1948 she was transferred to British and Irish, but returned to Burns and Laird in 1952 as the second LAIRDSCASTLE and worked the Irish cattle routes until 1957 when she was laid up in Glasgow.

A long spell of inactivity was broken only when she had a star role in *A Man Called Peter*, a film about the life of Peter Marshall, Chaplain to the US Senate which starred Richard Todd and Jean Peters. Although chartered for days, LAIRDSCASTLE's appearance on film lasted just seconds. She was broken up at Hendrik-ido-Ambacht in Holland during 1958. *[Middle: D.B. Cochrane, World Ship Photo Library]*

FIRST WORLD WAR STANDARDS (continued)

LADY PATRICIA (top), **KERRY COAST**
(middle) and **KERRY** (bottom)

*Caledon Shipbuilding and Engineering Co.
Ltd., Dundee; 1919, 1,391gt, 282 feet
T. 3-cyl. by Caledon Shipbuilding and
Engineering Co. Ltd., Dundee*

Burns and Laird lost no ships due to hostile action during the Second World War, but had their share of collisions, that involving KERRY COAST having unforeseen effects on the war effort.

She was completed as WAR SPEY in April 1919, and shortly afterwards bought by the British and Irish Steam Packet Co. Ltd. who renamed her LADY PATRICIA. When LADY names were dropped in 1938, she became KERRY, making it easy for Coast Lines Ltd. to rename her KERRY COAST when they formally acquired her in 1939. Transfer to Burns and Laird followed, without change of name, in November 1941.

On 11th March 1944, whilst leaving Liverpool for Waterford with general cargo including salt and barley, KERRY COAST was in collision with the Norwegian motor vessel MOSDALE (3,022/1939) near the Prince's Landing Stage. Holed in the engine room, KERRY COAST drifted upriver and, after her crew had been taken off by a tug, three other tugs nosed her into the beach just off the Number 6 Slipway of Cammell Laird's yard (middle photo). This proved to be a most unfortunate position, at least for the shipyard who were in the process of launching from this slipway a number of landing craft, LCT(3)s which were needed for Operation Neptune in a couple of months' time.

The Mersey Docks and Harbour Board started salvage work almost immediately, but on the 22nd March KERRY COAST's bow plating collapsed and 150 tons of permanent, concrete ballast moved and burst through the plates. This meant that number 1 hold could not be made watertight,

thus she could not be parbuckled upright, and camels were needed to refloat her. But not enough camels were available at Liverpool to meet the estimated 3,000 ton capacity needed to lift her. It was not until

6th May that the KERRY COAST was brought upright, and two days later was moved about 60 feet from Cammell Laird's wall. On 20th May - presumably a spring tide - she was raised and placed on Tranmere Beach.

The invasion of Normandy could not be held up by the KERRY COAST, but fortunately Cammell Laird were able to slew their launching ways so that the remaining LCTs would clear the wreck as they entered the Mersey.

KERRY COAST, 25 years old and badly damaged, was abandoned to the underwriters who paid out over £67,000, and her registration was closed. But H.P. Lenaghan of Belfast, who made something of a speciality of buying old and damaged ships, acquired and had her repaired, giving her the name BANGOR BAY. In 1946 she returned to Burns and Laird, this time to become KERRY once again, but a year later moved to the British and Irish Steam Packet Co. Ltd. Her adventures now over, she steamed on into her fortieth year, arriving at Passage West on 27th June 1959 to be broken up by Haulbowline Industries Ltd.

LADY EMERALD (top), **KILDARE** (middle) and **LAIRDSFORD** (2) (bottom)
Caledon Shipbuilding and Engineering Co. Ltd., Dundee; 1919, 1,389gt, 271 feet
T. 3-cyl. by Caledon Shipbuilding and Engineering Co. Ltd., Dundee
Coast Lines and its subsidiaries bought a total of five First World War standard ships, although the two built by Swan, Hunter - the first WESTERN COAST and the BRITISH COAST - were sold in 1922. The three Caledon-built examples gave remarkably long service, each passing through Burns and Laird ownership at least once.

WAR GARRY went to British and Irish Steam Packet Co. Ltd. in 1919 as LADY EMERALD. She was renamed CARLOW in 1938, and then BRITANNY COAST when she passed to Coast Lines Ltd. in 1939. In 1946, although coming under Burns and Laird ownership, she was given the British and Irish name KILDARE and operated in the livestock trade along with KERRY and

MEATH. Such were the complexities of Coast Lines that she was back under British and Irish ownership from 1948 until returned to Burns and Laird in 1952 and given the name LAIRDSFORD. In April 1960 she was broken up at Troon by the West of Scotland Shipbreaking Co. Ltd. *[Top: World Ship Photo Library; middle: D.B. Cochrane, World Ship Photo Library; bottom: Fotoflite incorporating Skyfotos]*

GLASGOW-LONDONDERRY
LAIRDS LOCH

Ardrossan Dockyard Ltd., Ardrossan; 1944; 1,530gt, 263 feet

Two 8-cyl. 4SCSA Atlas Polar oil engines by British Auxiliaries Ltd., Glasgow driving twin screws

Associated with the Londonderry-Glasgow service for most of her career, LAIRDS LOCH was built during the Second World War when this passenger service was, in fact, suspended. She emerged as a cargo and livestock carrier, her passenger accommodation being completed only in August 1946. Despite her yacht-like appearance, LAIRDS LOCH was not held in high esteem by the travelling public. During the summer months she was altered to carry passengers only. Her main deck was cleared and rows of basic seating provided: think of 12 hours on a hard seat on a lively vessel going round the north of Ireland!

LAIRDS LOCH made three round trips per week, with extra runs at the Fair Holiday weekends; and remained on the Londonderry passenger service until it closed in 1966. After three years, during which she did some Glasgow-Dublin sailings, she was sold to Israeli operators and as HEY DAROMA ran an eight-hour, thrice-weekly "cruise" service from Eilat to Sharm el Sheikh until 3rd September 1970, when attacked by Arab frogmen. Damaged by a mine, she was run ashore in the Gulf of Aqaba and became a total loss. *[Bottom: A. Duncan]*

PAPER TRANSFER
LOCH ALINE (top) and **SAINT FINTAN** (bottom)

Scott and Sons, Bowling; 1904, 208gt, 137 feet
C. 2-cyl. by the Barrow Shipbuilding Co., Barrow-in-Furness new in 1878

The LOCH ALINE was transferred to Burns and Laird in April 1946 and sold in October 1947, spending much of this period laid up at Ardrossan. Only a paper transfer, she is nevertheless included not just for completeness, but because her career before and after Burns and Laird ownership was so interesting.

As PLOVER she was built for David MacBrayne, and was fitted with an engine and boiler from their FLOWERDALE (488/1878). PLOVER carried passengers and cargo out of Oban, Mallaig and Kyle of Lochalsh until 1934, when she emerged from refit at Ardrossan looking more like a yacht, and with the name LOCH ALINE. During the Second World War she was based at Rothesay as an examination vessel, and the upper photograph shows her in wartime.

After her short and immobile Burns and Laird career, LOCH ALINE was sold to Thomas Heiton and Co. Ltd. of Dublin

for £3,500, over twice her book value. She underwent a radical rebuild into a cargo ship: as SAINT FINTAN she was one of the smallest colliers to have engines amidships. But this heroic conversion was short-lived,

and SAINT FINTAN arrived at Llanelly on 2nd July 1951 to be broken up by Edgar Rees Ltd. Her engine was now 73 years old.
[Both: Ballast Trust]

SECONDHAND CARGO SHIPS

LAIRDSOAK (2) (top)
T. van Duivendijk's Scheepswerf N.V., Lekkerkerk, Holland; 1937, 606gt, 163 feet
6-cyl. 2SCSA oil engine by Atlas-Diesel A/B, Stockholm, Sweden

With the end of the Second World War came the heady days of boom and Burns and Laird's virtual monopoly of the Scotland to Ireland services. The Belfast shipyards were busy, and in 1946 two large-hatched coasters, the LAIRDSOAK and LAIRDSROCK, came into the fleet exclusively to handle the vast steel trade into Harland and Wolff's shipyard.

LAIRDSOAK was Dutch-built, but for a British owner, William Wilson of Southampton, who was something of a pioneer of the motor coaster amongst British owners, taking delivery of her as NGARUA. Coast Lines were themselves early converts to the economies of the diesel coaster, and bought her from Wilson in 1939 for their Merchants Line Ltd., renaming her SILVER COAST.

After 14 years in Burns and Laird ownership, LAIRDSOAK moved within the group to Zillah Shipping Co. Ltd. of Liverpool who renamed her GARTHFIELD for their tramping operations. After her disposal by Zillah in 1962 she had various Greek owners under the names KRIOS, KYRIAKOULA K and DIMITRIOS II, but her fate is not known: *Lloyd's Register* deleted her in 1992 for lack of information.

LAIRDSROCK (2) (bottom)
Hawthorn, Leslie and Co. Ltd., Newcastle-upon-Tyne; 1935, 471gt, 166 feet
7-cyl. 4SCSA oil engine by Humboldt-Deutzmotoren A.G., Köln-Deutz, Germany
1957: 6-cyl. 4SCSA oil engine by Klöckner-Humboldt-Deutz A.G., Köln-Deutz, West Germany

Tyne-Tees Steam Shipping Co. Ltd. came into the Coast Lines Group in 1943, but were already convinced users of motor coasters, being faithful to Tyneside builders with the GLEN. She became BELGIAN COAST in 1946 as the new owners exerted their liking for uninspired corporate naming schemes, and in 1947 passed to Burns and Laird as LAIRDSROCK. A new engine in 1957 extended her life in the fleet until 1966, when the inevitable Greek owner bought her. As GIORGIS, LEFTERIS D and TENARON S she worked the eastern Mediterranean until 10th December 1980 when she grounded off Karpathos Island and subsequently sank.

DENBIGH COAST (top) and **LAIRDSFERN** (bottom)

N.V. Industrieele Maatschappij 'De Noord', Alblasserdam, Holland; 1937, 484gt, 163 feet 8-cyl. 4SCSA oil engine by Humboldt-Deutzmotoren A.G., Köln-Deutz, Germany

In the late 1930s Coast Lines Ltd. went to Holland for several motor coasters including the DENBIGH COAST. She came into the fleet of Burns and Laird Lines in 1952 as a replacement for LAIRDSFERRY and was renamed LAIRDSFERN. She is seen discharging at Belfast with a traction engine on the berth.

After seven years LAIRDSFERN went back to Coast Lines and her old name, DENBIGH COAST. She met her end on 18th July 1960 when, outward bound from Manchester to Belfast, she was in collision with IRISH MAPLE (6,218/1957) in the Mersey. She sank within ten minutes, fortunately without loss of life. [Top: A. Duncan; bottom: World Ship Photo Library]

POST-WAR CATTLE SHIPS

LAIRDS MOOR (this page) and **MIRNA** (opposite top)

Wm. Denny and Brothers Ltd., Dumbarton; 1948, 990gt, 256 feet

8-cyl. 2SCSA oil engine by Sulzer Brothers Ltd., Winterthur, Switzerland

LAIRDS MOOR and her sister LAIRDS BEN were built to cover cargo and cattle sailings throughout the Coast Lines Group's Irish trades. The name LAIRDSMOOR had been used before, but the name of the new motor ship was spelt LAIRDS MOOR.

She passed to Belfast Steamship Co. Ltd. in 1960, although given the name COLEBROOKE which was a traditional one for the Belfast, Mersey and Manchester Shipping Co. Ltd. Trade was buoyant enough for her to

be lengthened by Grayson, Rollo and Clover Ltd. at Birkenhead in 1963. In 1970 she was sold to Yugoslavia, becoming MIRNA, and on 1st December 1984 was scuttled off Nerezine, Mali Losinj, Yugoslavia. *[Opposite top: World Ship Photo Library]*

LAIRDS BEN (middle) and BROOKMOUNT (bottom)

Wm. Denny and Brothers Ltd., Dumbarton; 1949, 995gt, 264 feet
8-cyl. 2SCSA Sulzer oil engine by William Denny and Brothers Ltd., Dumbarton

After ten years with Burns and Laird, LAIRDS BEN went to the Belfast, Mersey and Manchester Steamship Co. Ltd. as BROOKMOUNT in 1959. This company, whose history is told in *Ships in Focus Record 3*, had long been a thorn in the side of the Belfast Steamship Co. Ltd., but soon after the transfer of LAIRDS BEN the smaller company was absorbed by its bigger rival.

As was her sister, BROOKMOUNT was sold in 1970, subsequently carrying the names IKARIA, PIERRE RODOLPHE, ZIAD and SWEET WAVES. Her end was not particularly sweet, as on 19th November 1983 she sank after being shelled during the Lebanese Civil War whilst laid up at Tripoli, Lebanon, and was broken up *in situ*.

POST-WAR CATTLE SHIPS
(continued)
RATHLIN (top), **LAIRDSCRAIG** (middle) and
GLENGARIFF (bottom)
*Alexander Stephen and Sons Ltd., Linthouse;
1936, 1,599gt, 273 feet*
*T. 3-cyl. by Alexander Stephen and Sons Ltd.,
Linthouse*

Built as RATHLIN for Clyde Shipping Co.Ltd. in
1936, this vessel was acquired by Burns and
Laird in 1952 and renamed LAIRDSCRAIG in
June 1953. RATHLIN had an illustrious war
service, and as a convoy rescue ship was
responsible for saving many lives. Bunks
were constructed on her erstwhile cattle
deck, together with a sick room, operating
theatre, and increased messroom, cooking
and toilet facilities. She was equipped with a
fast motor boat; and given increased bunker
capacity, sand ballast, and empty drums to
add buoyancy. RATHLIN completed no less

than 24 round voyages in convoy, of which six
were to Russia, including PQ17 which lost 24
ships when the convoy was ordered to
scatter. A grand total of 634 personnel
rescued from 13 ships was the highest
number recorded by any rescue ship.

In May 1956 LAIRDSCRAIG was
transferred from Burns and Laird to the City
of Cork Steam Packet Co. Ltd. who renamed
her GLENGARIFF to replace their KENMARE
on the Liverpool-Cork service. On 30th
December 1963 she made the very short
journey to Passage West, Cork to be broken
up by Haulbowline Industries Ltd. *[Top and
bottom: World Ship Photo Library]*

POST-WAR PASSENGER SHIPS
IRISH COAST

Harland and Wolff Ltd., Belfast; 1952, 3,324gt, 340 feet
Two 10-cyl. 2SCSA oil engines by Harland and Wolff Ltd., Belfast driving twin screws

The IRISH COAST has a slightly tenuous place in the history of Burns and Laird: she did spend significant periods on their services, although she was never in their ownership or colours.

IRISH COAST was built as a spare to relieve each of the seven similar vessels of Coast Lines subsidiaries whilst they were away on winter overhaul. In summer she was intended to run for Burns and Laird on the Glasgow-Dublin service but, when the SCOTTISH COAST was built, IRISH COAST ran on the summer-only daytime service from Ardrossan to Belfast, replacing the veteran LAIRDS ISLE. IRISH COAST returned to the

Glasgow-Dublin service in 1965 and in several subsequent summers.

Like so many of her predecessors, IRISH COAST found a second career in Greek ownership. In 1968 she was sold to the Epirotiki Steamship Navigation Co. 'George Potamianos' S.A., Piraeus and was renamed ORPHEUS, but within a year she had also carried the names SEMIRAMIS II, ACHILLEUS, and APOLLON XI, which was

rendered APOLLON 11 in 1980. Epirotiki Lines sold her in 1981 and she was renamed REGENCY. Her end was somewhat inglorious. In November 1984 she was laid up at Batangas in the Philippines, and on 11th October 1989 was driven aground there in a typhoon and seemingly was abandoned by her, no doubt debt-laden, owner. *[Fotoflite incorporating Skyfotos]*

POST-WAR PASSENGER SHIPS (continued)

SCOTTISH COAST (opposite all), **GALAXIAS** (top and middle) and **PRINCESA AMOROSA** (bottom)

Harland and Wolff Ltd., Belfast; 1957, 3,817gt, 330 feet

Two 10-cyl. 2SCSA oil engines by Harland and Wolff Ltd., Belfast driving twin screws

The SCOTTISH COAST has a special place in this book as, although she did not carry a Burns and Laird name, she was the last passenger ship on their best-known service between Glasgow and Belfast. In line with her name, she was delivered to Coast Lines Ltd., and registered in Liverpool. She wore the funnel colours of the Belfast Steamship Co. Ltd. on trials, because she was due to relieve that company's ULSTER MONARCH which was going for a four-month overhaul. She is seen in these colours in the top photograph on the opposite page, taken 21st March 1957. In July 1957 SCOTTISH COAST transferred to the Glasgow-Dublin service of Burns and Laird, being registered in their ownership from November 1957 and repainted in their colours, which she wore continuously until 1969. She was really too big for the needs of this service, and only ran at full capacity for a short period in the summer, but many a winter's night she sailed with more crew than passengers. She was reduced to two round trips a week in winter months, and so was idle for three days each week. She remained on the Glasgow-Dublin service until 1965, with the exception of a period in October 1961 when she relieved the British and Irish ferry MUNSTER (4,148/1948) on Liverpool-Dublin sailings after the Irish ship had been damaged in collision.

After 1965 her service record was more disjointed. For several summers she ran between Ardossan and Belfast, for which a car lift was installed forward and removed in the winter when she returned to Glasgow-Belfast sailings. In the roll-on roll-off era, SCOTTISH COAST was something of an anachronism, and it is salutary to remember that, within 24 hours of her maiden voyage, the Atlantic Steam Navigation Co. Ltd. were launching their roll-on roll-off BARDIC FERRY (2,550/1957).

After 1966 SCOTTISH COAST also relieved Belfast Steamship vessels on Liverpool-Belfast sailings and had periods on Glasgow-Belfast sailings. Ownership reverted to Coast Lines in November 1968, although she still worked the Glasgow-Belfast route during the next summer. Her final sailing on 30th September 1969 was both her last for Coast Lines, and the last on the historically very important route between Scotland and Northern Ireland, all traffic being diverted to the Ardrossan-Belfast car ferry LION.

In November 1969, after a short lay-up at Birkenhead, SCOTTISH COAST was sold to the Kavounides Shipping Co. S.A., Piraeus and was renamed GALAXIAS (top), being used for cruises in the Mediterranean. In 1986 she went to Vancouver for use as a floating hotel, but got into financial trouble and was sold to Cyprus-based operators in 1989. Next year

she re-entered service after being extensively rebuilt, and is still in service as PRINCESA AMOROSA.

SCOTTISH COAST was the thirteenth and last of a line of twin-screw motor ferries delivered to Coast Lines by Harland and Wolff to a basic design that had originated with the ULSTER MONARCH of 1929. By the 1950s, the design was definitely dated, as the lack of drive-on, drive-off facilities showed. But there can be no doubt as to the soundness of their build, as PRINCESA AMOROSA - still in service with her original engines - testifies. *[Opposite top: B.L. Devenish-Meares; this page top Paul Boot; bottom Jim McFaul]*

THE LAST CATTLE CARRIER

LAIRDSGLEN (2) (opposite and top) and
DEVON EXPRESS (bottom)

*Ardrossan Dockyard Ltd., Ardrossan; 1954,
1,544gt, 298 feet*
*Two 6-cyl. 2SCSA Sulzer oil engines by
George Clark (1938) Ltd., Sunderland driving
twin screws*

The last ship built for Burns and Laird, this
large cargo and cattle carrier was mainly
employed on the Glasgow-Dublin service.
She had 12 derricks and could carry 750
tons of cargo together with 480 head of
cattle, this number rising to 528 after
alterations. When the cattle trade
demanded, she made occasional trips to
Birkenhead from Dublin, and sometimes
loaded Dublin cargo overside from one of
United States Lines ships which had
diverted to Glasgow and missed its Dublin
call. In 1969 she went to Manchester for
conversion to a pure cattle carrier
(opposite) and in this capacity made runs
to North Africa, the Black Sea, and one
trans-Atlantic trip to Texas. From 1st
October 1971 she was owned by P&O Short
Sea Shipping, and then from 28th
September 1973 by Belfast Steamship Co.
Ltd. In March 1974 LAIRDSGLEN was sold
to her oft-times charterer, Frans Buitelaar,
who had made great inroads into the Irish

cattle trade to the detriment of Burns and
Laird and the other cross channel
operators, and initially remained under the
red ensign as DEVON EXPRESS. After
spells under the Liberian (bottom, taken
18th May 1976), Panamanian, and
Philippine flags, she was sold to Spanish
shipbreakers and arrived at Cartagena on
9th December 1983. *[Opposite: Fotoflite
incorporating Skyfotos]*

UNIT LOAD CONVERSIONS
POINTER (2) (top)

Ardrossan Dockyard Ltd., Ardrossan; 1956, 1,265gt, 224 feet

7-cyl. 2SCSA oil engine by George Clark and North Eastern Marine (Sunderland) Ltd., Sunderland

The POINTER and SPANIEL originated in mistakes made by Coast Lines' coastal tramping subsidiary, Zillah Shipping Co. Ltd. Having achieved some success with small motor vessels in the early 1950s, Zillah directors were keen to move into bigger coasters, and persuaded the parent company to let them invest in the BIRCHFIELD and BRENTFIELD. But on delivery Zillah quickly found that they had made an expensive mistake, the long-lived post-war shipping boom was finally over, and there were too many vessels of this size chasing too few cargoes. But Coast Lines management baled them out, and in 1958 the ships were taken in hand for conversion to unit load carriers to handle containers, trailers and flats. BIRCHFIELD became POINTER, a traditional Burns' name, although ownership remained with Coast Lines Ltd. and they operated on Irish Sea routes not associated with Burns and Laird, notably Belfast to Preston and to Liverpool, trading as Link Line.

At the beginning of 1965 the POINTER and SPANIEL were transferred to Burns and Laird Lines Ltd., but do not seem to have traded in their colours. This was just the first of a variety of transfers which saw them passed around what was now the P&O group and owned under whatever company was administratively convenient. For POINTER, this ended in 1975, when sold to the almost inevitable Greek owner who named her TAURUS III. Although sold for breaking up at Eleusis in 1981, and reported as such in one well-researched work on P&O, in fact she was reprieved and subsequently ran under the Honduras flag as LARNACA TOWN and MINA. Breakers at Perama, Greece finally caught up with her in May 1986.

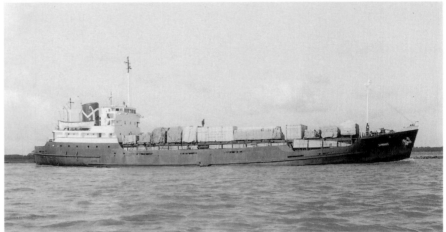

SPANIEL (3) (middle) and **CONISTER** (bottom)
George Brown and Co. (Marine) Ltd., Greenock; 1955, 1,263gt, 224 feet
7-cyl. 2SCSA oil engine by George Clark and North Eastern Marine (Sunderland) Ltd., Sunderland
SPANIEL, originally Zillah's BRENTFIELD, had a career that exactly paralleled that of POINTER until October 1973. She then became yet another one-time Burns and Laird vessel to be sold late in life to the Isle of Man Steam Packet Co. Ltd., for whom she became CONISTER. In September 1981, after a mercifully brief sojourn under the Panama flag, she arrived at San Juan de Nieva, Spain to be broken up.

LATER STEEL CARRIERS
SYLVIAN COAST (top) and **LAIRDSBURN** (2) (bottom)

Hawthorn, Leslie and Co. Ltd., Newcastle-upon-Tyne; 1936, 513gt, 165 feet
7-cyl. 4SCSA oil engine by Humboldt-Deutzmotoren A.G., Köln-Deutz, Germany

1959: 6-cyl. 4SCSA oil engine by Klöckner-Humboldt-Deutz A.G., Köln-Deutz, West Germany

A near sister to LAIRDSROCK (2), LAIRDSBURN was a later transfer to Burns and Laird, arriving in 1959 from Tyne-Tees, for whom she had worked on the east coast as BEAL and later SYLVIAN COAST. Again, re-engining kept her in service until 1966, when she was disposed of to Greek owners. Subsequent names were AGIA SOFIA, FRIENDSHIP III and ARIADNE. On 5th March 1978 she hit a breakwater at Augusta, Sicily in bad weather and sank. *[Top: A. Duncan]*

LATER STEEL CARRIERS
(continued)
LAIRDSFIELD (opposite)

*N.V. Scheepswerf Gebroeder van der Werf,
Deest, Holland; 1953, 504gt, 174 feet
8-cyl. 4SCSA oil engine by Motorenfabriek
D. en J. Boot 'De Industrie', Alphen a/d Rijn,
Holland*

In 1966 the steel boats working from
Greenock to the Harland and Wolff shipyard
in Belfast needed to be replaced and Zillah's
GREENFIELD and FOXFIELD were selected
for this trade, the former having been the
Dutch-owned COOLSINGEL. The general
manager of Burns and Laird asked for
suggestions for names for these ships. On
arrival at the Belfast shed at Lancefield Quay
one morning he found that some docker had
pencilled in the names HEEDRUM and
HODRUM. These suggestions were quite

apt, given the large number of highland and
island men in the crews. However, the
names LAIRDSFIELD and LAIRDSFOX were
the winners.

After alterations, notably to hatch
covers and coamings, the two ships settled
into service, but early in 1970 a fall in steel
traffic meant that only one ship was needed.
LAIRDSFIELD was put on the spot charter
market, but on 6th February 1970 having
sailed from Middlesbrough for Cork and
Passage West with a full cargo of steel
plates and columns, she rolled over within
an hour of sailing and sank with the loss of
ten crew. Later that month she was
refloated, as seen on the opposite page,
and was broken up at Middlesbrough by
Tees Marine Services Ltd. *[Opposite top:
Fotoflite incorporating Skyfotos]*

FOXFIELD (middle) and LAIRDSFOX (bottom)

*N.V. Ferus Smit v/h Firma J. Smit and Zoon,
Foxhol, Holland; 1952, 563gt, 189 feet
6-cyl. 4SCSA oil engine by N.V. Werkspoor,
Amsterdam, Holland*

Another of Zillah's Dutch purchases,
FOXFIELD was named LEEMANS until 1955.
Burns and Laird acquired her for the steel
trade and renamed her in 1966. The
LAIRDSFOX was the last ship to carry a
LAIRDS- name and funnel colours of red
basic with blue band and black top which
was introduced with the Royals in 1936.

She also had the distinction of
outliving Burns and Laird, and in September
1973 her owners became Belfast Steamship
Co. Ltd. In 1977 she was sold to Panama and
renamed LILAIDA, being broken up at Cadiz
in September 1989 after a period of lay-up at
Gibraltar. *[Top: Fotoflite incorporating
Skyfotos, bottom: World Ship Photo Library]*

THE LAST ROAR

LION and **BARONESS M** (opposite bottom)
Cammell Laird and Co. (Shipbuilders and Engineers) Ltd., Birkenhead; 1967, 3,333gt, 364 feet
Two 12-cyl. 4SCSA oil engines by Crossley Brothers Ltd., Manchester driving twin screws

It was a fitting gesture that the very last ship built for Burns and Laird should carry not one of the soulless LAIRDS- names, but one in the tradition of the senior constituent, G. and J. Burns. Oddly, however, Burns had never used the name LION. The roll-on, roll-off ferry was built for the Ardrossan-Belfast daylight service, and had a capacity for 1,200 passengers and 160 vehicles. She was designed to carry freight on trailers and lorries, and Northern Ireland Trailers - another Coast Lines subsidiary - was responsible for filling her with freight. Her launch on 8th August 1967 (opposite top) sounded the last post for the old Glasgow-Belfast service, although it was to be almost two years before it finally died. The photograph above shows her running trials.

LION's speed of 20 knots was similar to that of predecessors ADDER, VIPER and LAIRDS ISLE, and the schedule she maintained was broadly similar, but LION also took night sailings to and from Larne. The Ardrossan-Belfast route, on which Burns and Laird and its successor had invested so heavily, was to prove their last. Competition from the much shorter Stranraer-Larne crossing, especially for traffic originating in England, was too great, and in 1976 LION was transferred within P&O and rebuilt at Le Havre to run between Dover and Boulogne under the title Normandy Ferries. Burns and Laird ownership had been terminated in 1973, and during her subsequent 12 years' service within P&O she was to have at least six different registered owners, although she kept her name (this page bottom and opposite middle).

Sale in 1985 saw LION go under the Cypriot flag as BARONESS M, although she returned to the English Channel in the summers of 1987 and 1988 when she was chartered by British Channel Islands Ferries Ltd. to run as PORTELET. BARONESS M is still reported to be afloat in 1999, a reminder of a once-great company's last, lion-hearted attempt to compete on a sea crossing where it once had an almost-unassailable monopoly. *[Opposite bottom: Jim McFaul]*

SLOAN TRANSFERS

WESTERN COAST (top) and **TAY** (upper middle)

Goole Shipbuilding and Repairing Co. Ltd., Goole; 1951, 782gt, 234 feet

7-cyl. 2SCSA oil engine by British Polar Engines Ltd., Glasgow

By the late 1960s, the names of historic companies like Burns and Laird meant so little to the owners of their Coast Lines' parent that ships running on other companies' services were registered in their ownership. Some of the last ships to be 'owned' by Burns and Laird Ltd. were therefore these three motor vessels of William Sloan and Co. Ltd., which ran between Glasgow and Dublin, Belfast and the Bristol Channel in Sloan's colours and services. None had originated with Sloan, who in fact never built themselves a motor ship, and TAY began life as Coast Lines' WESTERN COAST, the fifth of the name. She was transferred to Sloan and renamed in 1958, and came to Burns and Laird in 1965. The next few years saw Sloan's Irish Sea cargo liner services succumb to roll-on, roll-off competition, and in 1968 TAY was sold to Panama as CHARALAMBOS. In 1973 she briefly became ERIKA, but on 14th May that year struck a rock off Roubos Island, near Ayios Evstratios, and later sank in shallow water. She was on a voyage from Galatz to Hull with a cargo of timber. *[Upper middle: World Ship Photo Library]*

TALISKER (lower middle)

George Brown and Co. (Marine) Ltd., Greenock; 1955, 1,016gt, 248 feet

8-cyl. 2SCSA oil engine by George Clark (1938) Ltd., Sunderland

The TALISKER came to Sloan in 1963, having been built for the Belfast Steamship Co. Ltd. as ULSTER PIONEER. Ownership by Burns and Laird from 1965 came to an end in 1968 when Coast Lines Ltd. took her over, but she was sold within a year. As BAT SNAPIR she ran under the Israeli flag, then became the Panama-registered WOODBINE, and finally the HONG SHEN of Singapore. Her polyglot career ended on 7th November 1988 when she sank off North Borneo after developing leaks.

KELVIN (bottom)

A. and J. Inglis Ltd., Pointhouse; 1955, 979gt, 252 feet

8-cyl. 2SCSA oil engine by George Clark (1938) Ltd., Sunderland

Formerly ULSTER PREMIER, KELVIN was a sister to TALISKER, and the two ships' careers ran in parallel until 1968. It is interesting to note that her builders had, many years previously, been one of Burns and Lairds' regular suppliers.

On sale by Coast Lines Ltd. in 1968, KELVIN became first the VASSILIA, then ALFTAN and TACAMAR III, all under the Panama flag. Her last owner, who renamed her CANAIMA, was based in Venezuela, but she ended her days in Colombia, being broken up in the port of Cartagena in 1983.

Top: a propellor for the QUEEN ELIZABETH 2 (65,863/1969) being discharged at Clydebank.
Bottom: a more mundane cargo is loaded onto the LAIRDSGLEN at Anderston Quay, Glasgow: Hillman Imps completely knocked down (CKD) for the short voyage to Dublin. Cargo like this, which would involve lengthy assembly in Ireland, makes the roll-on, roll-off revolution hardly surprising.

Top left: walk-on, walk-off traffic - Irish cattle being discharged at Merklands Lairage, Glasgow.

Top right: an older generation of vehicle being handled; note the slings and the spreaders to avoid damage to the bodywork.

Bottom: this coach seems to have been used exclusively to advertise the accelerated service provided by ROYAL ULSTERMAN and ROYAL SCOTSMAN in 1936. With advertising panels occupying the window spaces, any passengers would have had to put up with a dark interior.

INDEX OF SHIPS

All ships mentioned are listed. Names in capitals are those carried by ships in photographs.
(fc=front cover; fep and rep=end papers)

LAIRDS ISLE makes a smoky departure from Ardrossan on 9th July 1951. *[Michael Crowdy World Ship Photo Library]*

MAGPIE leaves Glasgow wearing the old Laird Line funnel colours, used by Burns and Laird Lines Ltd. between 1922 and 1929.